Carving the Nose & Mouth

By Jeff Phares

Fox
Chapel Publishing Co. Inc.
1970 Broad Street • East Petersburg, PA 17520 • www.foxchapelpublishing.com

Carving the Nose and the Mouth is a brand new work, first published in 2002 by Fox Chapel Publishing Company, Inc. The patterns contained herein are copyrighted by the author. Artists may make three copie of the patterns for personal use. The patterns themselves, however, are not to be duplicated for resale or distribution under any circumstances. This is a violation of copyright law.

Publisher   Alan Giagnocavo
Project Editor   Ayleen Stellhorn
Cover Design   Keren Holl
Desktop Specialist   Alan Davis
Step-by-Step Photography   John A. Brookins

ISBN #1–56523–161–9

To order your copy of this book,
please send check or money order
for the cover price plus $3.00 shipping to:
Fox Books
1970 Broad Street
East Petersburg, PA 17520

Or visit us on the web at
www.foxchapelpublishing.com

Printed in China

Because carving wood inherently includes the risk of injury and damage, this book cannot guarantee that creating the projects in this book is safe for everyone. For this reason, this book is sold without warranties or guarantees of any kind, express or implied, and the publisher and author disclaim any liability for any injuries, losses or damages caused in any way by the content of this book or the reader's use of the tools needed to complete the projects presented here. The publisher and the author urge all carvers to thoroughly review each project and to understand the use of all tools involved before beginnin, any project.

Table of Contents

Carving an entire human face involves a lot of study. Based on the feedback I have received from the students who attend my carving seminars, I believe there is a definite need out there for a series of books focusing on isolated areas of the human face. The book you are holding, Carving the Nose & Mouth, is the first of three books that will provide an in-depth study of human features.

Why carve just a nose and a mouth? That's a good question; one that is probably best answered by you. Perhaps you are an experienced carver who has noticed that the anatomy of the face you recently finished carving doesn't look "quite right." Or perhaps you are an experienced carver who has never tried to carve a human face before. Or you may even be new to carving all together and need a starting point for learning about carving faces. In any case, you need to look at carving just a nose and a mouth as practice. Practice makes perfect—and it will help you to learn the process and to make your future carvings more realistic.

Two Faces

I have chosen to provide you with step-by-step instructions for two faces: one Caucasian and one Native American. By studying and comparing the steps involved in carving both faces, I believe you will learn and understand much more than simply following along with one carving demonstration.

The first demonstration covers carving the nose and mouth of a Caucasian subject; the second explains how to carve the same area on a Native American face. You will notice that the features of the Caucasian face are more delicate and more narrow than the features of his Native American counterpart. Much of this can be traced back to the underlying bone structures and muscle structures of the face. Some illustrations are provided in the last section of this book.

Before You Begin

First, along with the illustrations and photos in this book, you'll want to do your own study of reference material before you begin carving. Look for photos or models or

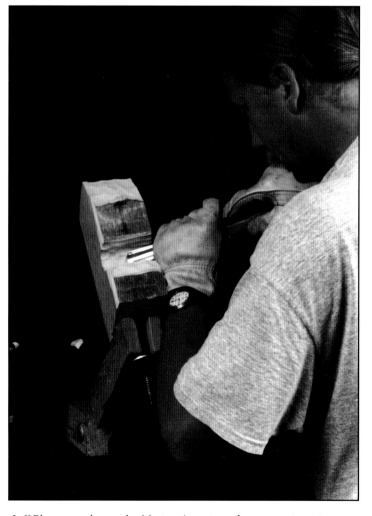

Jeff Phares works on the Native American demonstration piece.

other artwork of Caucasian and Native American faces. Get as close to your subject as you can. When I carve Indian busts and masks, I start with photos of Native Americans. I familiarize myself with the different characteristics of their faces: noses, cheekbones, eyes, lips, eyebrows... Even though we are just studying the nose and mouth in this book, all of these other features come into play.

Next, choose a piece of wood for your carving. I used basswood in the demonstrations. Why basswood? First, because the two faces are basically study sticks. Basswood is easy to carve and will give you a good feel for the gouge strokes. And second, because basswood photographed well. In the demonstration photos, we lit the pieces carefully so that the shadows will highlight the gouge cuts.

And last, assemble and sharpen the tools you'll need. Nothing will interrupt your creative flow more than having to search for and/or sharpen the right tool. Please note that I have been carving for years and have developed a liking for a number of specific tools. I use these tools repeatedly. You may have tools with which you are familiar. If those tools give you the same end result as the tools I use in the demonstrations, by all means, use them. It is not necessary to purchase a tool based on this book alone.

About Sharpening

As with any aspect of carving, I could go on and on; but for the purposes of this book, "simple" and "effective" are the two points to keep in mind when thinking about sharpening your tools. Regardless of the wood you're using or the subject you're carving, sharp tools are a necessity. As with anything, it is best to learn from the ground up. Learn to use a stone and a hand strop before you move on to other methods of sharpening your tools.

Getting Started

When you have chosen your wood and your tools are sharp, you are ready to begin carving. Apply the pattern to the block either by enlarging and tracing it or freehand. Take a second look at your reference material and review the gallery photos and anatomy illustrations in the book; then let's get started on carving the nose and mouth.

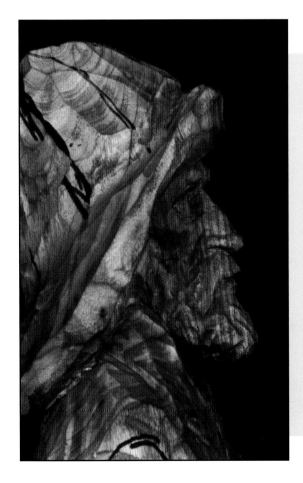

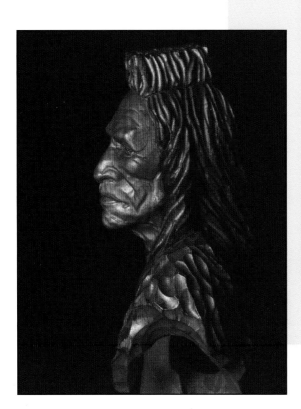

Caucasian
Front view of the
demonstration piece

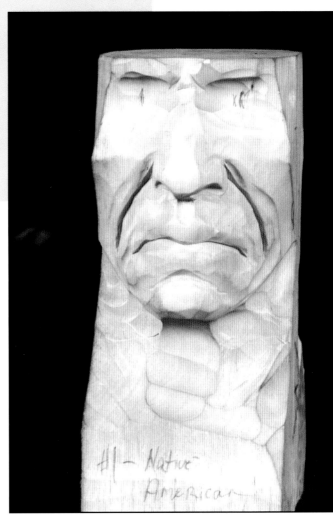

Native American
Front view of the
demonstration piece

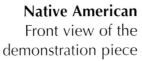

Now that you have studied the gallery photos and have a good visual in your mind of the differences between a Caucasian face and a Native American face, let's get started carving. Below are two photos of the finished pieces. Both are carved on small "ingots" of wood and are meant to be used as study sticks when finished. Only the noses and the mouths are carved so that we can focus on those areas specifically.

Again, before you begin, study these two photos carefully. Note the differences in the profiles. You will see major differences in the structures of the cheekbones, the brow ridge, the nose and the mouth. You will want to refer back to these photos frequently as you carve to make sure that your carving is on track.

Caucasian

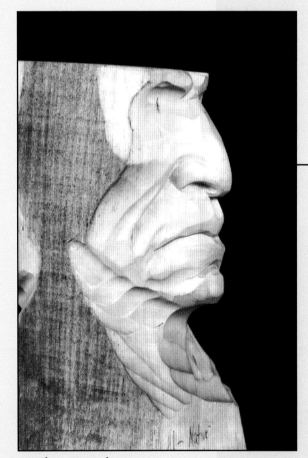

Native American

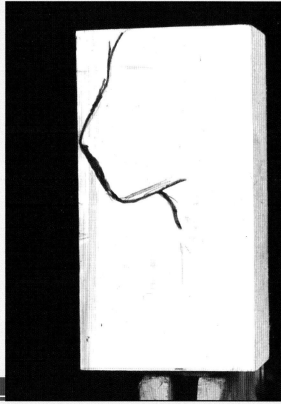

1

Use any size block of wood that has the proportions of a human face. This block is about three inches wide by six inches deep. Sketch the profile of a Caucasian man on the block. Use the anatomy information on page 64 for reference.

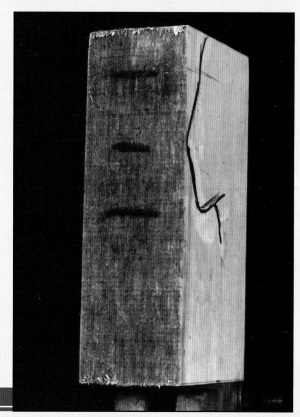

2

Mark the eyebrow, the nose and the bottom of the chin.

3

Using a #5, 30 mm gouge, remove the wood from the front of the block. Work all the way across the block, keeping your cuts straight.

4

Notice how the forehead has been set back from the end of the nose. Now, use a #9, 25 mm gouge to relieve wood from under the chin. Simply push the front of the neck straight back under the chin.

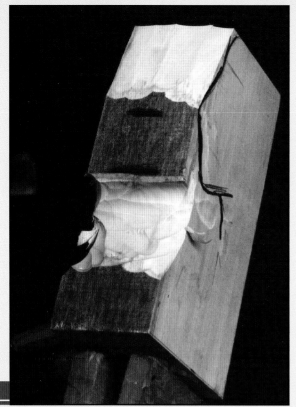

5 Start working up at an angle, knocking off the corners of the neck area.

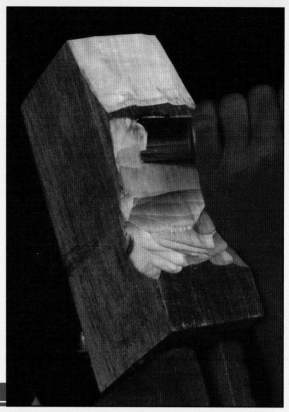

6 Using a #7 gouge, push the mouth barrel back. It is important to work all areas a little at a time so the entire face progresses at the same rate.

7 Notice how no wood has been removed at the tip of the nose area. That is the farthest reaching point on the face.

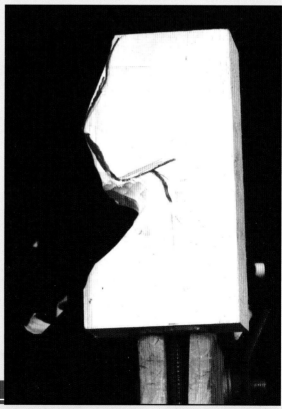

8 A photo of the side-view profile shows the progress to this point. It is important to think in basic shapes during the early stages to create a good, strong facial structure.

9

The next step is to block in the eye area. Draw in the eyebrow ridge—the ridge above the top part of the eye socket. Make sure you are marking where the bone lies, not where the hair of the eyebrows would be.

10

Using a #9 gouge, cut straight across the face directly under the line.

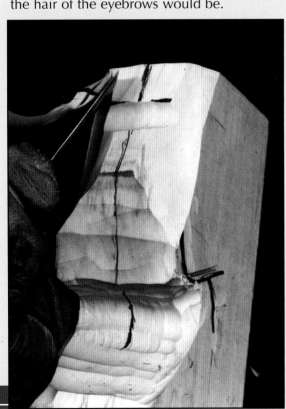

11

Using a #5, 30 mm gouge (a #3 or a #4 will work as well), knock back the cheekbones and the sides of the face.

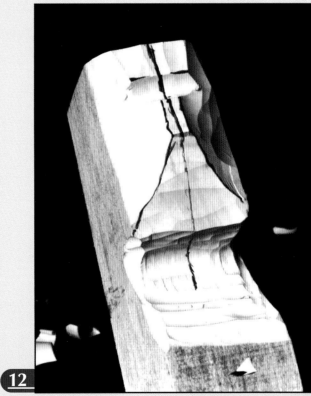

12

Draw in lines to mark the nose and the mouth area. Continue to remove wood from the sides of the face, getting closer to the chin.

13

A photo of the side view shows the progress at this point.

14

Use a #5, 30 mm gouge to work the mouth barrel and the bottom half of the face back. This will give the chin area an angle.

15

Still using the #5 gouge, work down the side of the jaw, pushing it back, too.

16

A side view shows how the face is pushed back and how the mouth and nose area have been brought out off the face.

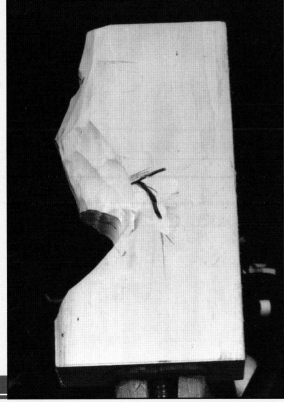

17

A view of the opposite side shows where the original jaw line and neckline were drawn in and how the cuts are positioned in relation to these lines.

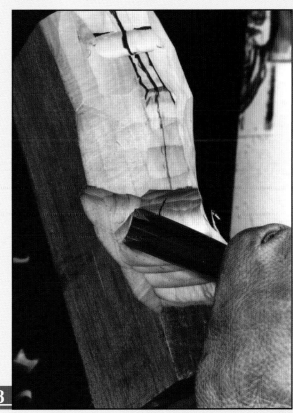

18

Work under the neck to establish the angle of the jaw.

19

Using a #9 gouge, push the neck back and create the three planes of the neck area—one to the front and one to each side.

20

The profile is starting to take shape. Notice how everything drops back into the face, bringing the nose and the mouth barrel forward.

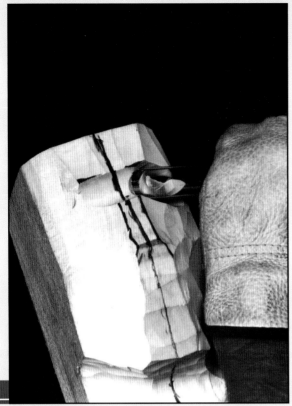

21 Use a #11 gouge to cut in the eye sockets.

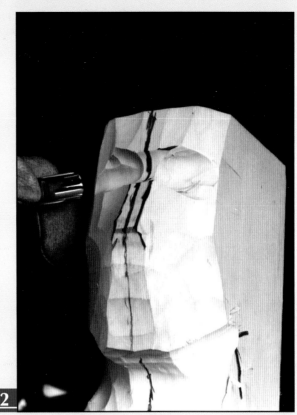

22 Do not cut right up to the centerline. Come out of the cut early to leave a little space there for the bridge of the nose.

23 A front view shows the formed and shaped eye sockets.

24 A side view of the carving to this point shows how the eye sockets are opened up, how the side of the cheek is pushed back, and how the nose and mouth barrel are brought out. Notice also how the bridge of the nose is coming into play here.

Carving the Nose and Mouth • 13

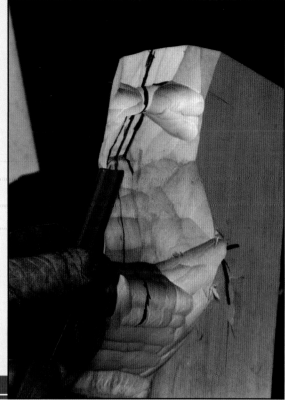

25

These next steps will establish the shape of the nose. Using a #7, 1/2-inch to 3/4-inch gouge, start the cut just under the tip of the nose.

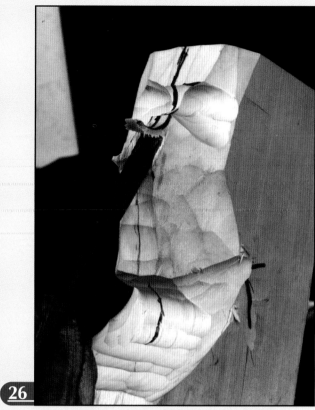

26

Turn the #7 gouge upside-down, with the concave surface facing the nose. Push the #7 right up to the ridge of the nose. This takes some force.

27

Notice how the gouge is digging in on the corners. This is exactly what should happen. Stop the cut at the bridge of the nose.

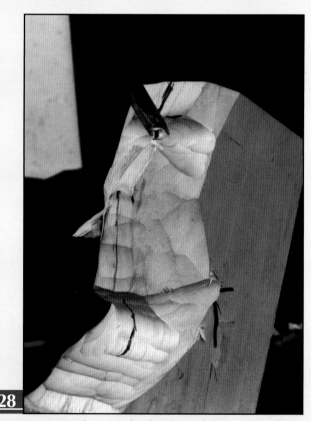

28

Create a dent in the bridge of the nose.

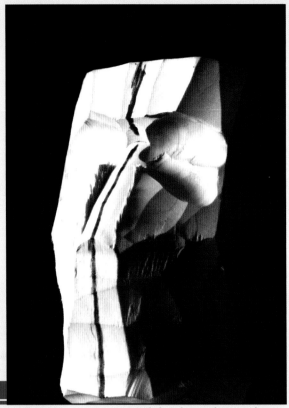

29

A three-quarter view of the face shows the cuts for the nose. Notice the shape of the front of the nose and how the tool corners have dug in, leaving an equal space on each side of the center line.

30

Next take the #9 gouge and split the forehead with a shallow cut.

31

Using a #2 gouge, tilt the forehead back, helping to create a stronger profile.

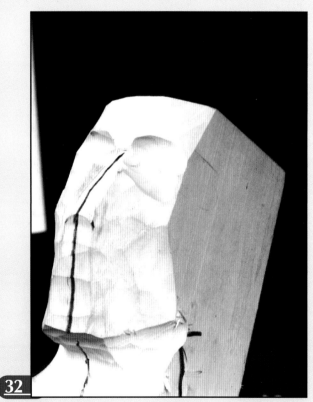

32

Notice how the forehead has a slightly backward slant to it now that Step 31 is complete.

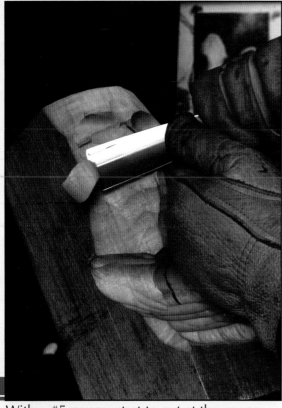

33

With a #5 gouge, start to cut at the gouge marks left on the side of the nose in Step 26. Sweep back along the side of the face from the nose. Strive to create a smooth transition from the nose to the cheek.

34

The area to the left of the centerline has been finished. Notice the difference from the right side of the face to the left.

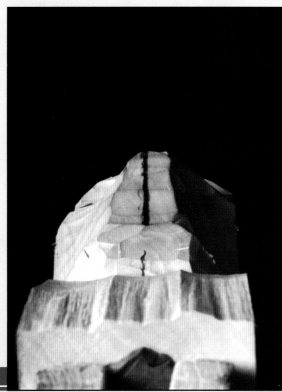

35

Looking up past the chin, you can see how the left-hand side of the face is pushed back quite a bit farther than the right-hand side. Each step will push the face farther back.

36

This side view shows how the nose and the mouth have been brought forward even more. The angle of the jaw has been established.

16 • Carving the Nose and Mouth

Dare to be different

By GENE BASS

DARE to be different. Be original. Walk to a different drummer. Being original and different may not be the only game in town. But if you want to aspire to new carving heights and go for the blue, being different sure is way ahead of whatever is in second place.

Is being different worth the extra time and effort it takes to develop your own original, different style? You better believe it is! Your carving is not a copy of someone else's work. No matter whether you are competitive or not, you have the satisfaction of knowing that your work is uniquely yours and yours alone. There are no other carvings quite like your carvings. You are not bound by someone else's standards. You are setting your own standards, free to explore, to achieve, and to improve. You are on the cutting edge, a leader instead of a follower.

People and judges are looking for something new and different — something original. If the carvings you enter in shows are no different from the others, no matter how good they are they get lost in the crowd. People and judges may find them, but they have to go looking for them. If your carvings are different and original, they will stand alone (even if they are mediocre) and shout, "Hey, look me over!" If everything is equal, different and original can mean the difference between best-of-show, first place, or second place. In fact, different and original may win over a better carved, but less imaginative, carving.

What do I mean by daring to be different? Let me count the ways. A carving should have some or all of these characteristics: (1) rhythm, flow, motion and action; (2) tell a story; (3) a base that is an integral part of the carving — see 1 and 2; (4) contrasting combination of carved surfaces; (5) a subject that is different from the majority of carved subjects; (6) stands out — if others carve closed-winged birds, then you carve open-wing birds; (7) originality; (8) artistic imagination; (9) pleasing to look at from all sides, unless a relief carving; (10) holds viewer's interest and attention, and never is boring.

Well, it's put up or shut up time. Let's take a look at some award-winning carvings that are different and exhibit some of the above characteristics, especially 7-10.

Last winter, I carved a carousel frog titled *Froggy Goes a Courtin'* (photo 1). His base is 32" long, and he stands 27" tall to the top of his hat. I believe that, all things being equal, bigger is better. Bigger not only stands out in a crowd, it is also easier to carve. It may be more expensive, but it may not be any more time consuming to carve. What's that? Did I say easier to carve and may not take longer to do? Bigger means the removal of more wood, and the removal of more wood requires larger tools to remove wood faster. The carving of fine detail is much less tedious

— Photos 2-7 courtesy of Vestal Press

Photo 2: Jack Portice's "Storyteller" shows how interesting contrasting carved surfaces can be.

Photo 3: "Mountain Thunder" by Jack Portice.

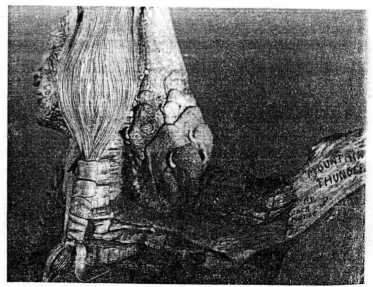

Photo 4: Side view of "Mountain Thunder" shows buffalo herd stampeding out at back of head.

Photo 1: The base is an integral part of "Froggy Goes A Courtin'" by Gene Bass.
— Photo by Gene Bass

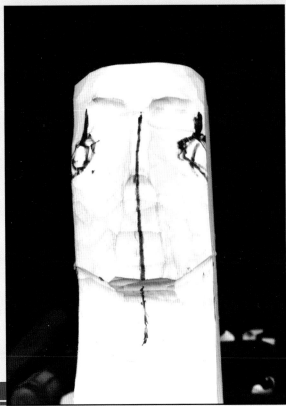

37

Draw a line to mark where the cheekbones will protrude. Notice that the cheekbones are not right under the center of the eye: They are off on the corners of the face.

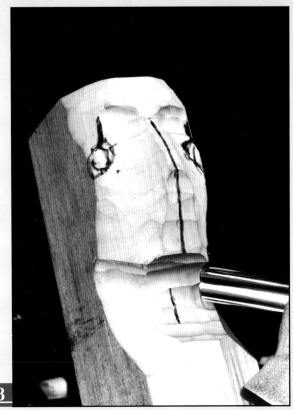

38

With a #11 gouge, clean up the chin and begin to set the jaw line. This step will finalize the length of the face. The outside shape of the face and the length of the face has to be set before the nose and the mouth are put in.

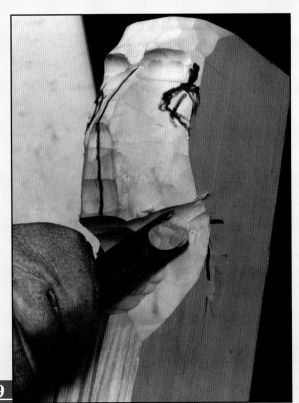

39

Set the sides of the jaw with a #9 gouge. Work back and forth between the left and right sides so both sides of the jaw progress at the same rate.

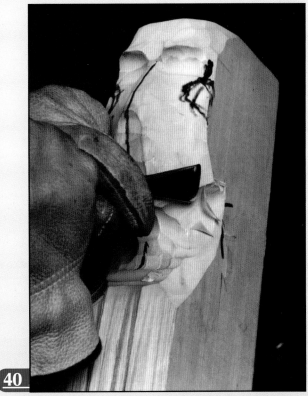

40

Work the corners of the jaw off with an upside-down #3 gouge. You'll notice that I have literally knocked some chunks off the front of the block below the neck to get the excess wood out of the way.

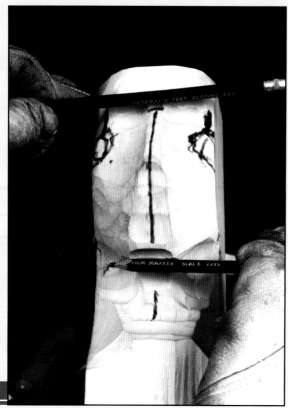

41 The bridge of the nose and the bottom of the chin are set. It's now time to establish where the bottom of the nose will fall. Proportion-wise, this should be halfway between the bridge of the nose and the bottom of the chin.

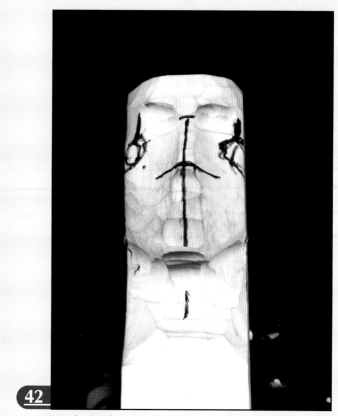

42 Mark the bottom of the nose.

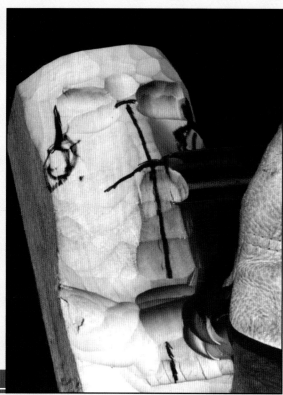

43 Using a #9 gouge, cut in at the edge of the nose just below the mark. Cut straight across this area to establish the bottom of the nose.

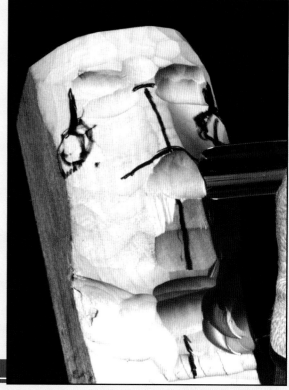

44 Continue to remove wood under the nose. As the bottom of the nose is formed, the mouth is pushed back.

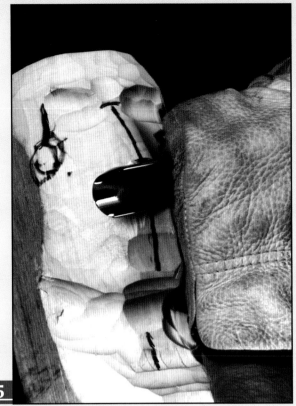

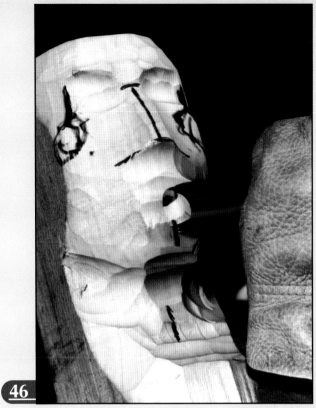

45 Be sure to follow through with the cuts.

46 Now that the bottom of the nose is established, push the mouth barrel back using a #9 gouge.

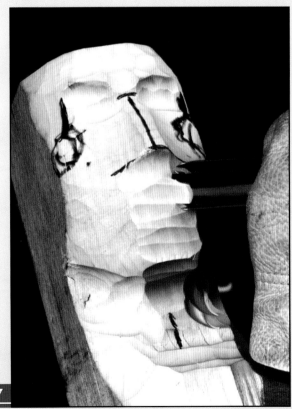

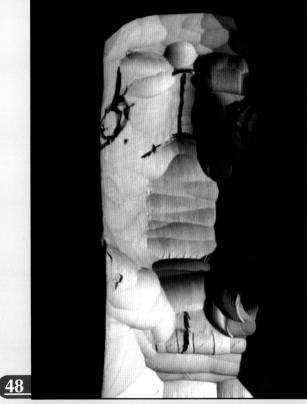

47 Make a number of smaller cuts straight across this area.

48 This front view shows the wood removed for the mouth barrel. Notice how the three planes of the face are starting to take shape.

49 Using the #5, 30 mm gouge, redefine the shape of the mouth barrel and round off the sharp corners.

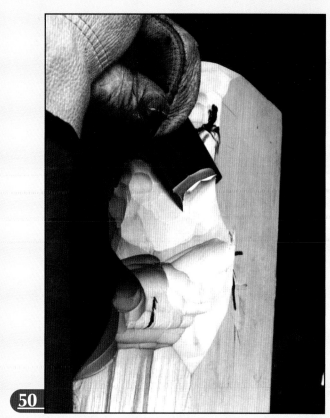

50 Begin to define the secondary profile. Make downward cuts under the cheekbone, along the natural hollow in the cheek.

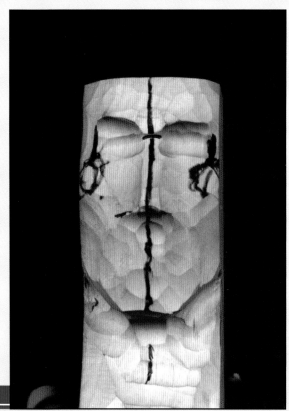

51 A front view of the piece shows the hollowed cheek areas. Notice the steeper angle around the mouth barrel and how the sides of the face drop back more to create a smooth transition of form.

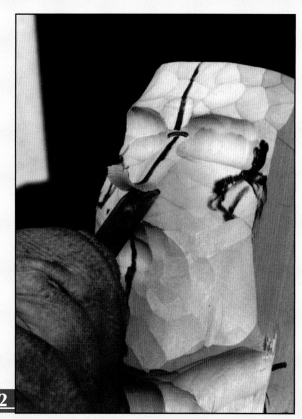

52 Now that the basic shape of the face is set, start to work on the nose. Turning a #7 gouge upside-down, slide the tool up to create the actual shape, or outer profile, of the nose.

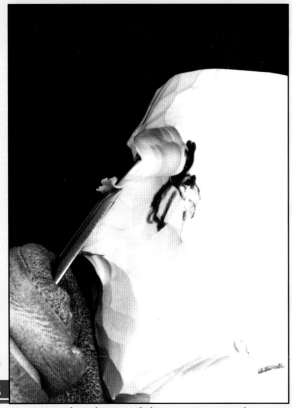

53

Creating the shape of the nose may take several passes with the #7 gouge.

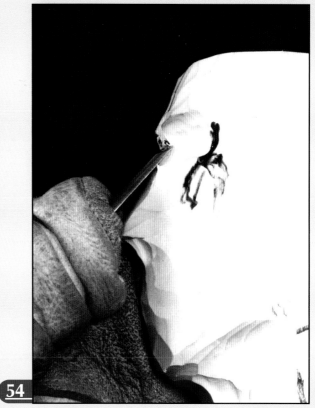

54

Push the gouge all the way up to the bridge of the nose.

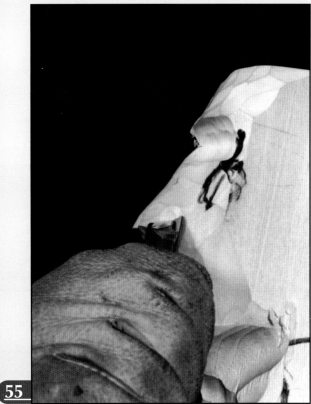

55

Isolate the ball of the nose, which is at the front end of the nose.

56

The cut should come up to this point, about halfway up the nose.

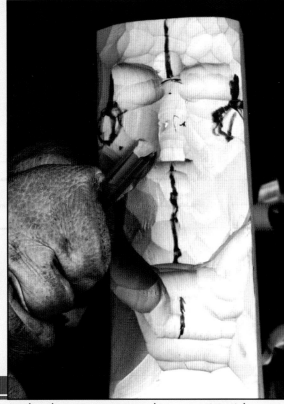

57

Make the same cut on the opposite side.

58

Notice how the nose and the mouth barrel have been brought forward and the eye sockets have been set back. The secondary profile is also taking shape (see page 64).

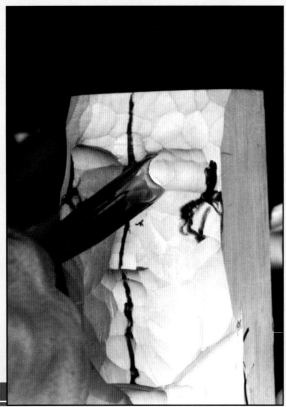

59

Refine the sockets and push them yet deeper into the face with a #9, 20 mm gouge. Notice how the plane of the eye socket is now almost straight across.

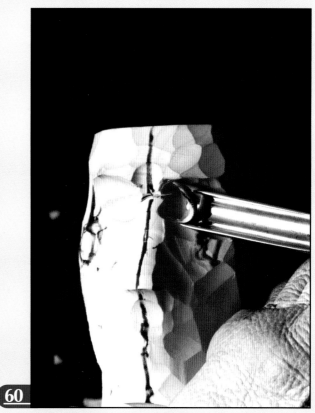

60

Cut in from the other side of the socket to create more depth.

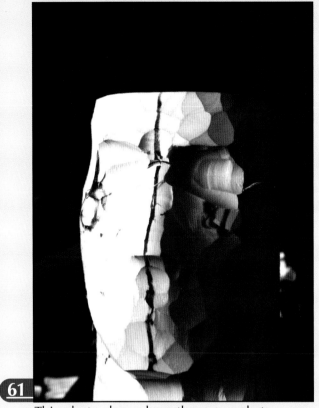

61 This photo shows how the eye sockets should be shaped at this point.

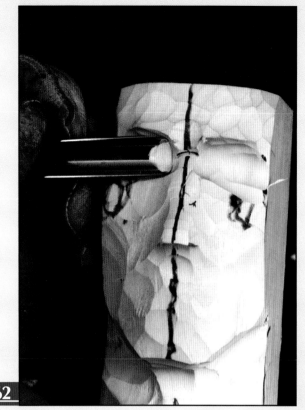

62 Refine and deepen the eye sockets. Cut more wood out of the inside corners than the outside corners.

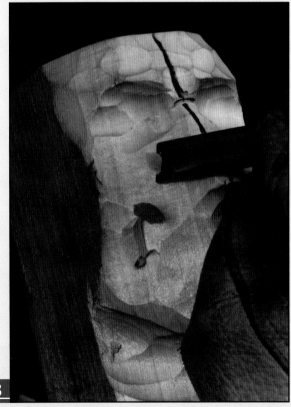

63 Blend the cheek and the area under the eye socket to make a smooth transition between the two. Notice how much of the black magic marker has been removed.

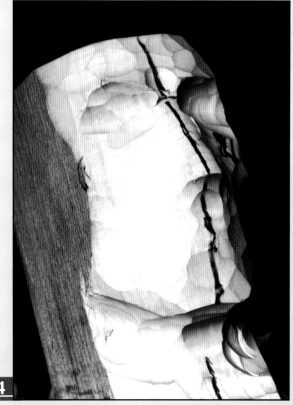

64 A photo at this point shows how much wood has been removed from the left side of the face.

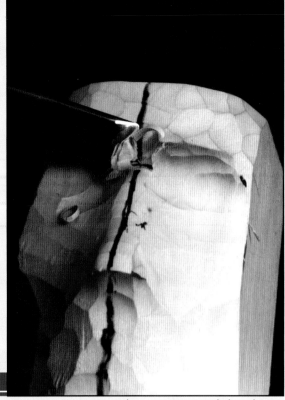

65

Using a #7, 1/2-inch gouge, round the sharp edges of the brow into the crease between the eyebrows. Work carefully; this is a tricky cut.

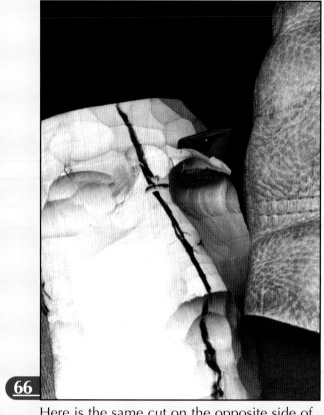

66

Here is the same cut on the opposite side of the face. The cut ends well before the black line.

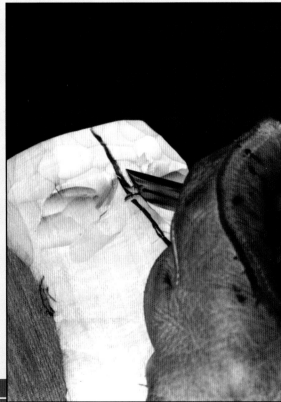

67

Take a little bit of wood off the side of the nose and right up to meet the cut you just made. This will create the crease in the brow, as shown on the left-hand side.

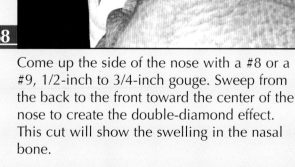

68

Come up the side of the nose with a #8 or a #9, 1/2-inch to 3/4-inch gouge. Sweep from the back to the front toward the center of the nose to create the double-diamond effect. This cut will show the swelling in the nasal bone.

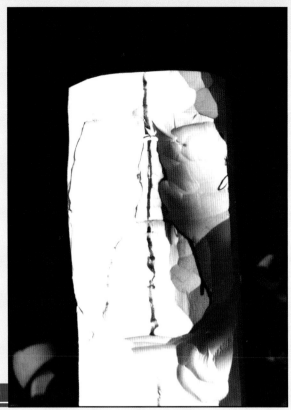

Draw the edges of the nose, mouth and eye areas.

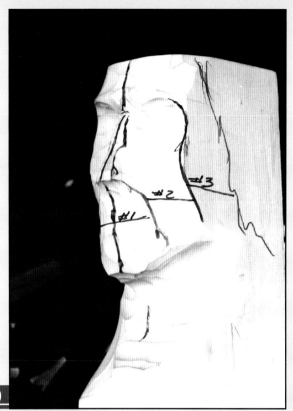

This three-quarter view shows the three planes of the face. Notice the ridges left by the gouges and the depth of the planes. Make sure the structure of the face to this point is accurate. All the detail in the world will not look right if the basic form of the face is incorrect.

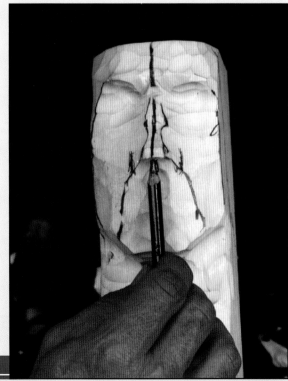

Mark the center of the nose with a pencil. Also pencil in the width of the nose. Try to make the marks equidistant from the center mark on the nose.

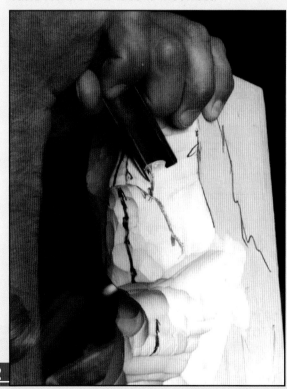

Using a #7, 5/8-inch or a little bigger gouge, remove some wood down toward the jaw line and back into the face. This will eliminate some wood around the back of the nose.

Caucasian

Carving the Nose and Mouth • 25

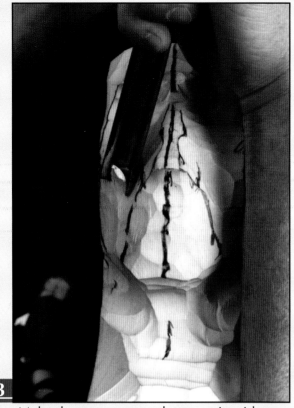

73 Make the same cut on the opposite side. This photo shows the approach.

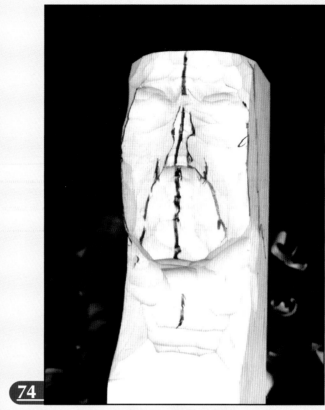

74 A front view shows the cuts.

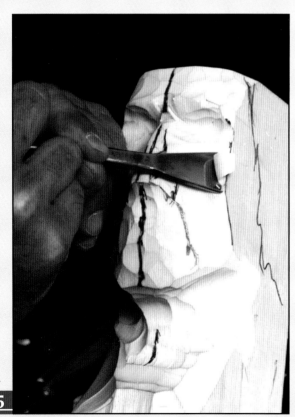

75 Cut down the cheek with a #3, 1-inch gouge, pushing the face back. This will make the second plane of the face stronger.

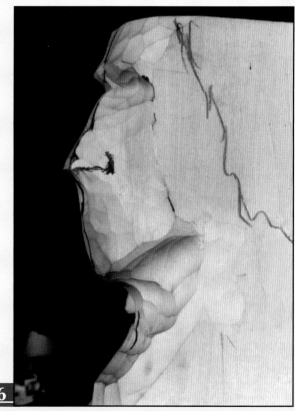

76 A side view photo shows the progress so far. Again, notice how much the face has been pushed back.

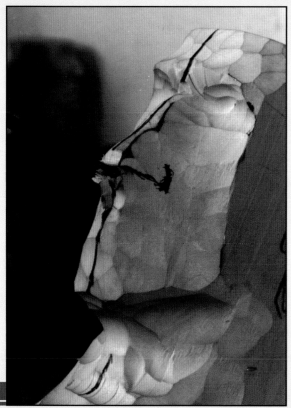

77

Start to set the nose into the face. Using a #7, 10 mm gouge turned upside-down, round down and over the end of the nose; then cut straight into the wood.

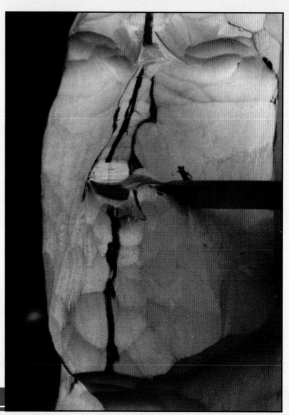

78

Now swing the tool around and rotate it right into the wood to create the bottom part of the nostril that wraps around the dental curve of the face. Notice the angle of the tool and how it is going down and away from the nose.

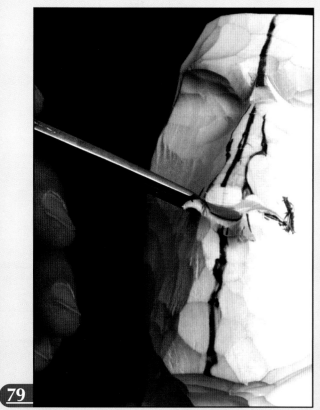

79

Make the same cut on the opposite side of the nose. This is the third cut that establishes the basic shape of the nose.

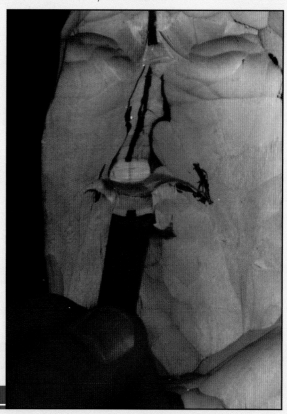

80

Using a #7 gouge, relieve wood from the end of the nose. Carefully cut up to, but not beyond the cuts you made in Step 79.

Caucasian

Carving the Nose and Mouth • 27

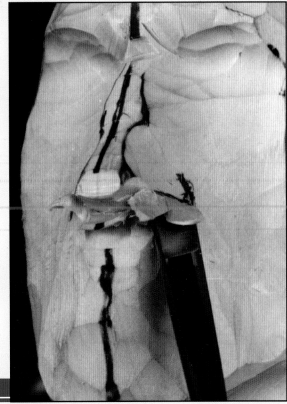

81

Relieve the sides of the nose. Notice how I am working on the side of the mouth barrel, not on the front. These cuts will create the three planes of the mouth barrel: the frontal plane and two side planes.

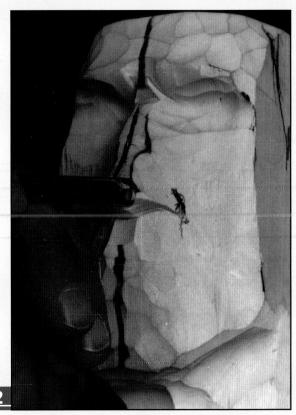

82

Turn a #5, 10 mm gouge upside-down to shape the wings of the nose.

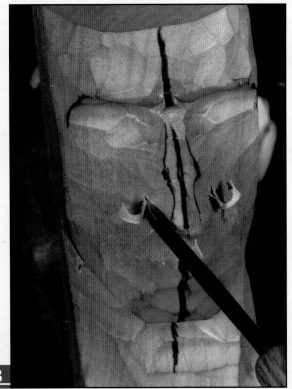

83

This photo, shot from above, shows the same cut. The cut on the right-hand side is finished.

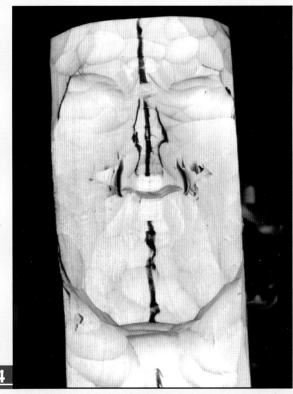

84

A front view of the piece shows the cuts completed. I have not relieved them yet so that you can see the shapes of the cuts and how wide they are.

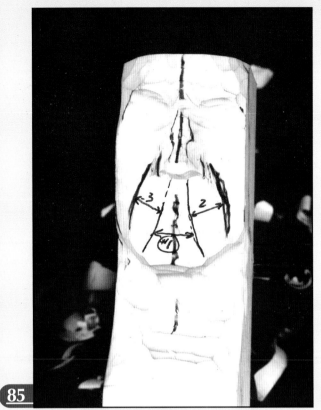

85 Draw in the outside lines of the mouth. Notice how I have drawn in the three planes of the mouth barrel.

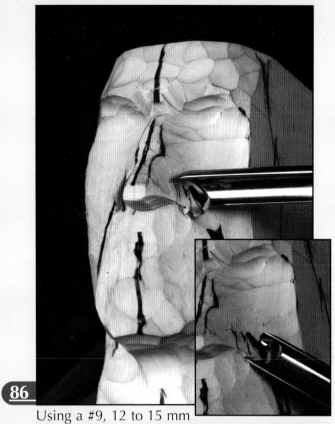

86 Using a #9, 12 to 15 mm gouge, cut in as shown in the inset photo. Rotate the gouge to conform to the shape of the side of the nose.

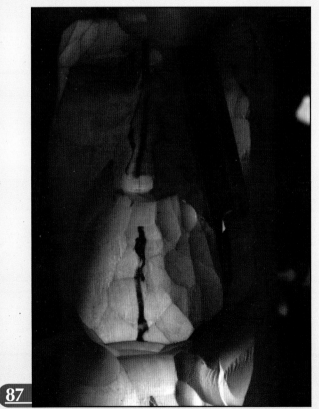

87 Cut down along the "smile lines" of the face with a #7, 5/8-inch gouge. The left side has already been cut.

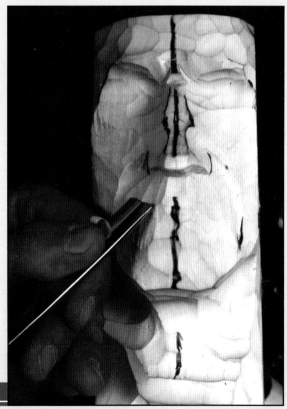

88 Using a #9 gouge, clean up the side of the mouth barrel, still maintaining the three planes.

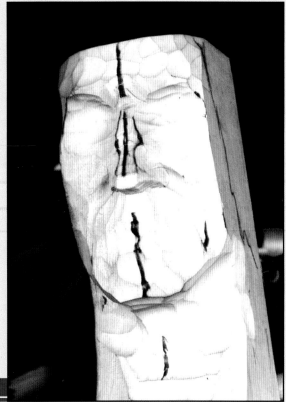

89

The cuts on both sides of the mouth are completed. Notice how the cuts block in the location of the smile lines.

90

The shadows in this photo show the depth and the amount of wood that has been removed. Notice how half the nose is off the face and half the nose is on, or into, the face.

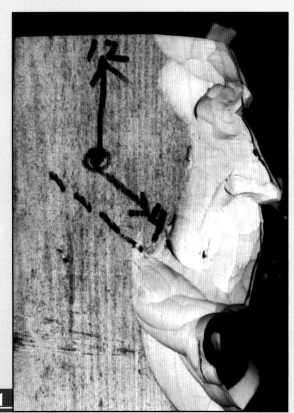

91

Draw the hands of a clock in the 4 o'clock position on the side of the face. The mark along the hour hand will show the angle of the jaw. Mark in the hands at 8 o'clock on the other side of the face.

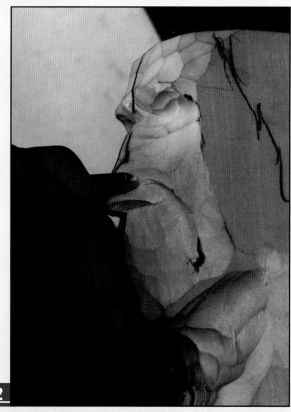

92

Using a #11, 5 mm gouge, make the cut along the side of the nostril. This cut rolls right down into the smile line.

30 • Carving the Nose and Mouth

93

This photo shows the cut. Notice how the cut sets the little crease that isolates the nostril and the wing of the nose from the rest of the nose.

94

A side view of the cut shows the progress to this point. Notice the pushed-back cheekbone, the shape of the eye socket and the orbit, and the shape of the mouth barrel.

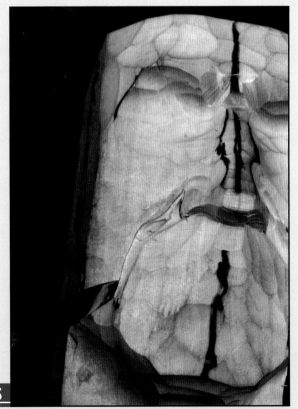

95

Using a carving knife, cut down the side of the face at about a 45-degree angle. The cut starts at the top of the nostril and goes right down through the gouge cut that was made in Step 87.

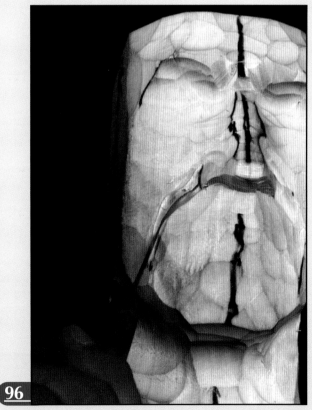

96

Lay the knife in along the same angle as the mouth barrel and relieve the cut. You will be slicing a thin piece of wood out of the cut.

Caucasian

Carving the Nose and Mouth • 31

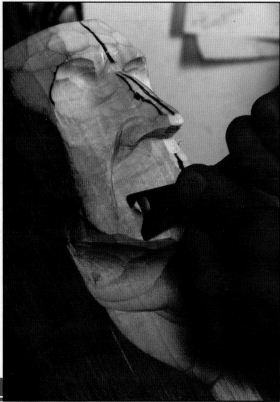

97

Now that the two smile lines are cut in, blend the mouth barrel back into the cuts. Use a #3, 1-inch gouge to remove wood in small bits. This will narrow the chin area at the same time.

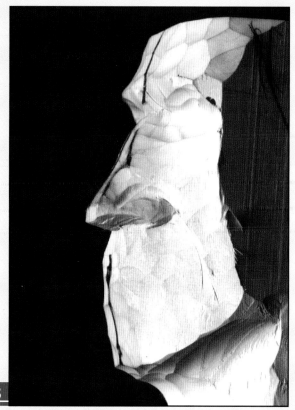

98

A side view photo shows the cuts. Notice how the mouth barrel is blended back into the smile line. If necessary, clean up the bottom edge of the nostrils with a #7, 10 mm gouge.

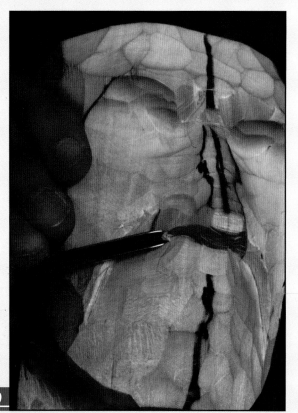

99

Using a #11, 3 mm gouge, cut in the nostril opening. Start the cut as shown here.

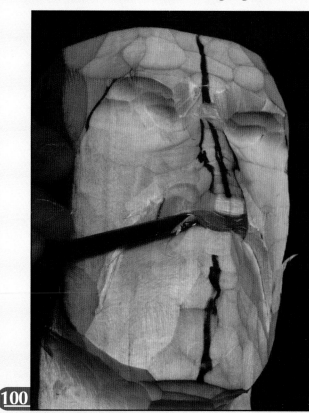

100

Midway through the cut, the gouge should be in this position.

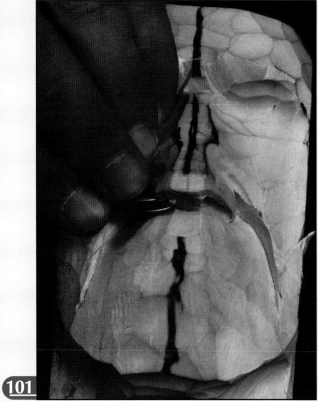

101 End the cut here. Scoop the gouge right out of the wood, leaving a little space of wood in place for the septum of the nose.

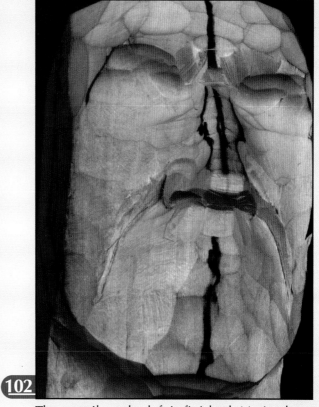

102 The nostril on the left is finished. Notice how thick the smile line fold is at this stage. You will thin it later.

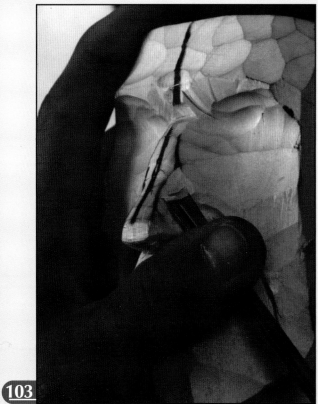

103 Using a #5, 8 to 10 mm gouge, soften the top edge of the nostril. Blend this area so it transitions into the shape of the nose. Also, clean up the hollow area in the narrow part of the nose below the nasal bone.

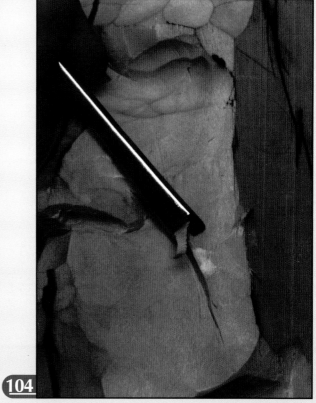

104 With just the corner of a #7 gouge turned upside-down, shave and round the sharp edge off the smile line.

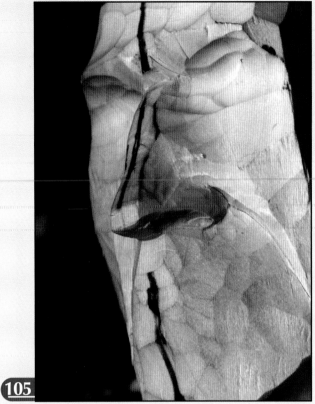

105

The nose at this point should look like this. Use a little v-tool to clean up the bottom area if necessary. Notice how the bottom edge of the nostril curls up back into the opening.

106

Round off the tip of the nose and the ball. Notice the little hourglass shape: That's the double-diamond effect.

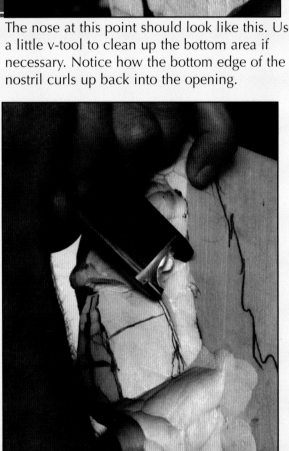

107

Mark in the guide lines for the planes of the mouth. Using a large #7 gouge, hollow out under the area where the cheekbones are in the natural hollow of the face.

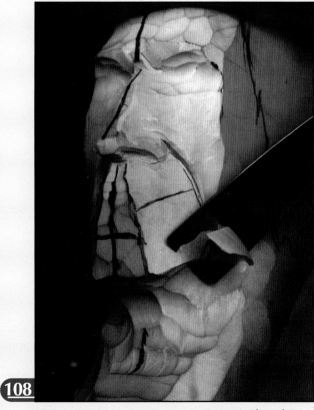

108

Using a #5, 30 mm gouge, narrow the chin. Trim the edge and round it over to blend the two areas together.

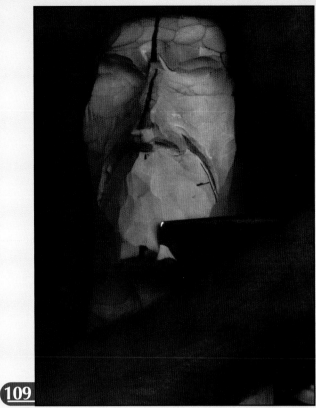

109 Flip the #5, 30 mm gouge upside-down to round the bottom point of the chin.

110 A side-view photograph shows the progress to this point. The typical hairline is drawn in to give you a better visual of the face. Notice where the sketch marks are. That's where the smile line is.

111 Using a #9 gouge, push the front of the neck back.

112 Work toward establishing the jaw and narrowing the neck. Note the amount of wood that has been removed from the neck and jaw area when compared to the photo for Step 110.

Carving the Nose and Mouth • 35

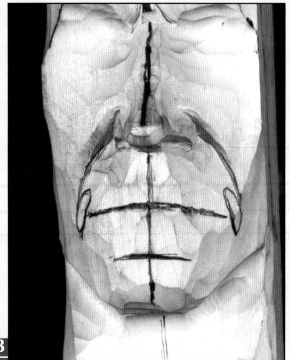

113

Once the chin and neck are cut in, notice how everything blends together nicely. Draw in the lines to show the proportions of the mouth. Measure from the bottom of the nose to the bottom of the chin and divide that area into three equal parts. The top horizontal line is the meeting of the lips themselves; the second horizontal line is the separation between the mouth and the chin. The two circles on each side of the mouth mark the two muscle groups at the ends of the mouth.

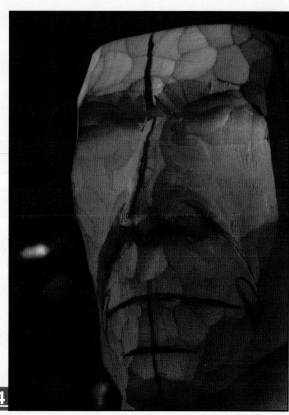

114

Use a #11, 10 mm gouge to cut in the small dent in the upper lip that leads to the nose.

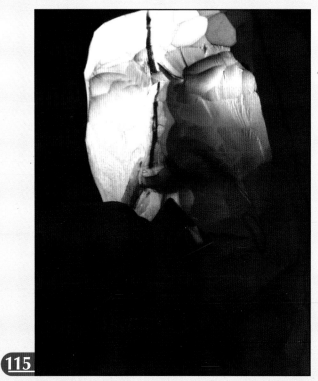

115

Blend and flatten the side of the mouth barrel. This area of the face should not remain flat.

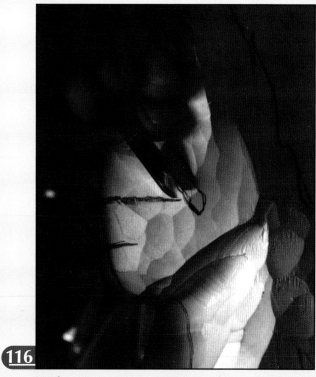

116

With a #11, 5 mm gouge, make a cut in front of the muscle group.

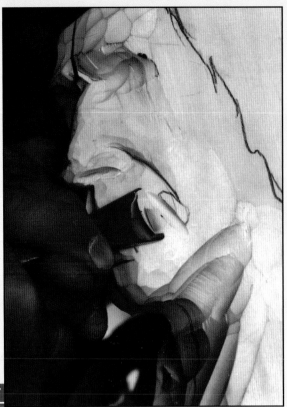

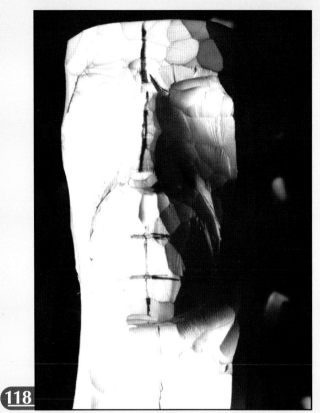

117 Use a #3, 1-inch gouge to remove wood from the mouth barrel back to the muscle group. Remove only enough wood to blend the two areas flush to the muscle.

118 Study the right side of the face. Notice how the cheekbone is higher; the muscle is lower; and the mouth barrel is lower yet. This stair-stepping effect is very important.

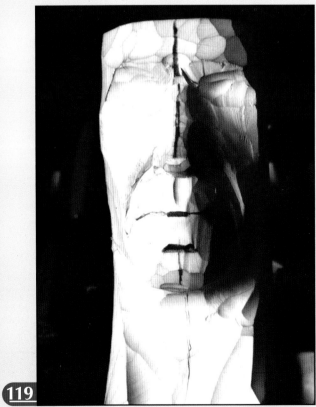

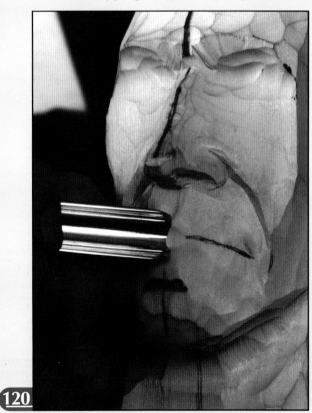

119 Blend all the areas together; then draw in the mouth line or lip line. Notice how the chin has been narrowed. Here again you can see the stair-step around the muscle on the corner of the mouth.

120 Using a #9, 15 mm gouge, carve in the indentation where the lips meet. Start at the center, carve right down to the muscle, and stop.

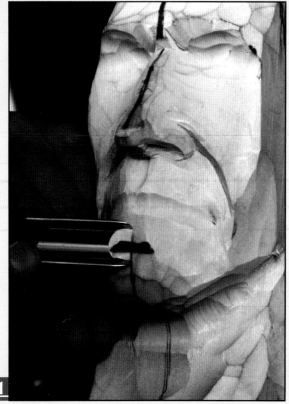

121

With the same gouge, separate the chin from the mouth area.

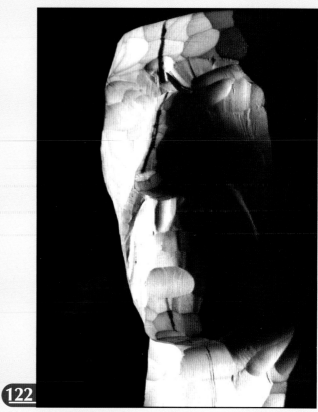

122

A three-quarter view photo shows the finished cut.

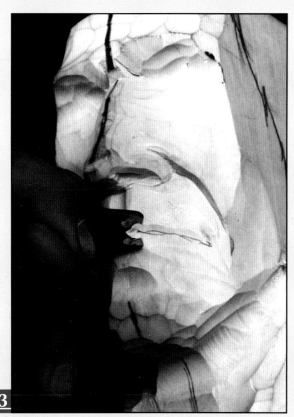

123

Mark and recut the lip line with a #13 wide-angle v-tool. Again, start in the center, cut to the edge, and stop.

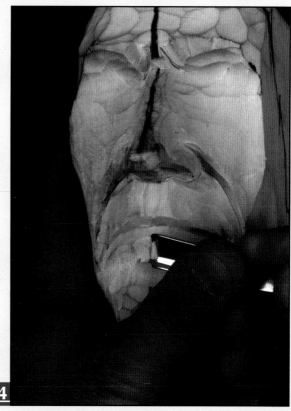

124

Use a #7 gouge to thin the edge of the bottom lip. Notice the edge of the top lip. That's the edge where the pink part of the lip meets the skin or flesh color of your face.

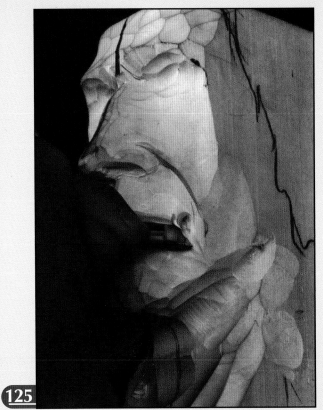

125

Use the corner of the gouge to make a cut that will establish and sharpen the edge of the lip where the bottom lip tucks underneath the top lip at the corner.

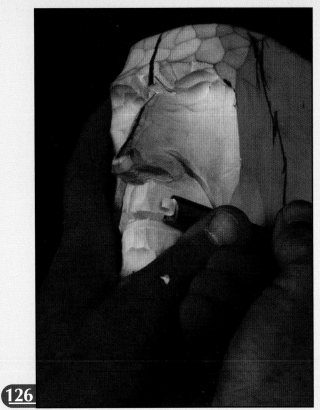

126

Start at the muscle and work toward the front of the face. Make sure your tool is extremely sharp. This is where you can thin or fatten the lips according to your design.

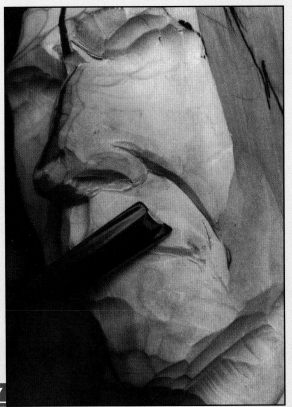

127

With the same #7 gouge, blend the top edge of the lip back into the mouth barrel, heading toward the smile line. Take little bits. Don't take big chips off at this stage.

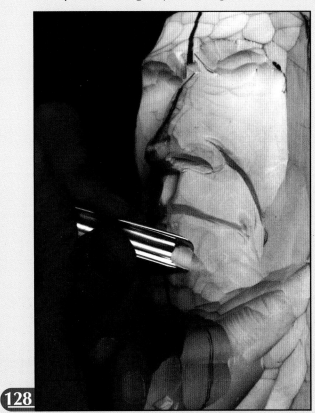

128

Using a #11, 10 mm gouge, deepen the separation between the chin and the mouth.

129 Round the chin up and blend some of the sharp edges with a #3, 1-inch gouge.

130 A side-view photo with heavy shadows shows the depth and shapes of the cuts. Notice how the edges of the chin have been rounded down. The chin is back just a little farther than the bottom lip, and the bottom lip is back just a little farther than the top lip. That's what creates the Caucasian profile.

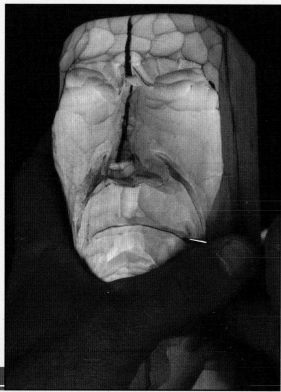

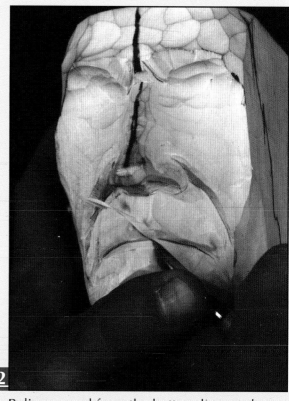

131 With a knife, open up the lips just a bit. Move the knife slowly in small strokes across the lip line.

132 Relieve wood from the bottom lip—underneath the top lip—to create a shadow. Cut from corner to corner, removing one chip of wood.

 *Caucasian*

40 • Carving the Nose and Mouth

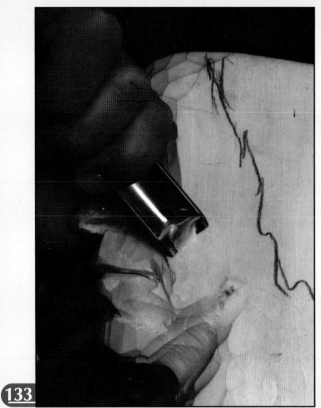

Using a #7 gouge, cut down the cheek to create the natural hollow under the cheekbone along the side of the face. This will form the natural hollow created by the muscle structure of the face.

This side view photo shows the finished cuts. Notice the shapes of the cuts and how everything blends together.

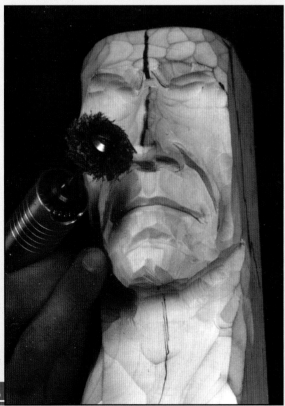

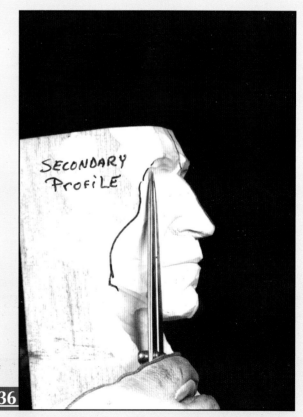

Soften the surface of the carving with a Scotchbrite pad attached to a flexible shaft tool. Be sure to use eye protection for this step. The pad will soften hard edges, blend structures and take off any dirt and pencil marks.

The finished nose and mouth. Compare the primary profile and the secondary profile: This face is definitely not flat! (See pages 6 and 7 for front and side views of the finished piece.)

Carving the Nose and Mouth • 41

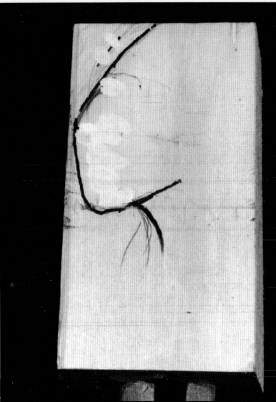

1 Draw the profile on the block. Compare this profile with the profile for the Caucasian subject (Step 1, page 8) and you'll note a number of differences, especially in the shape of the mouth and the eye region.

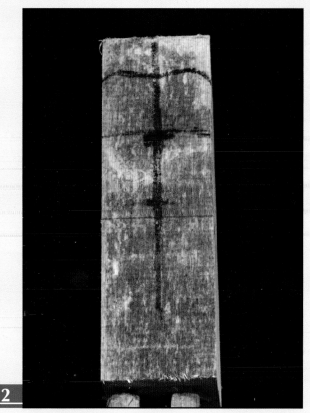

2 Mark in the brow ridge, the point of the nose and the chin on the front of the block.

3 Using a large, wide gouge and a hammer or mallet, start removing excess wood from the forehead area. Work in straight passes across the block from the point of the nose to the end of the block. These cuts will create the slant from the nose back to the forehead.

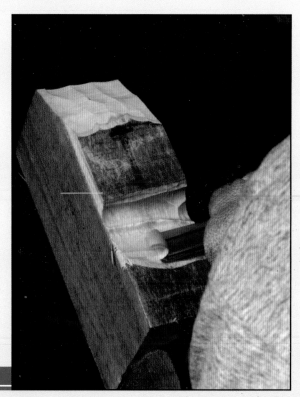

4 With a #9, 25 mm gouge, remove wood from under the chin and from the front of the chest. Remove additional wood to push the neck back.

42 • Carving the Nose and Mouth

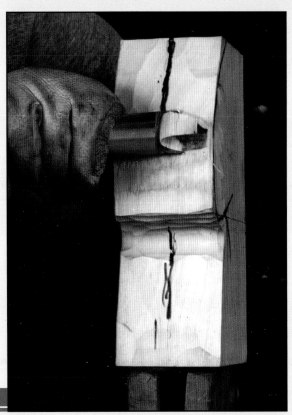

5

Start pushing the mouth area back to the profile line that you drew. Be sure to look at the piece from all angles as you work—the top of the head, up through the chin. You need to keep everything flat and square at this point. One side cannot be higher than the other.

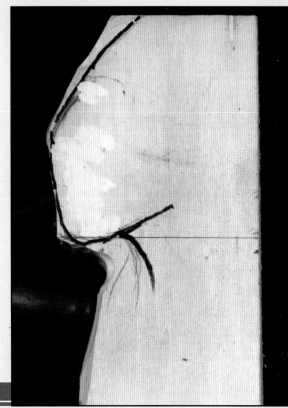

6

This side view photo shows how much wood has been removed. Note how far the face has been pushed back. It is important to think in shapes and masses as you go along, not in details just yet.

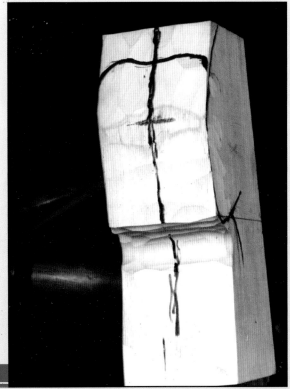

7

Draw in the brow ridge. This line roughly marks the edge of the bone—not necessarily the hair of the eyebrows. Remark the bottom of the nose.

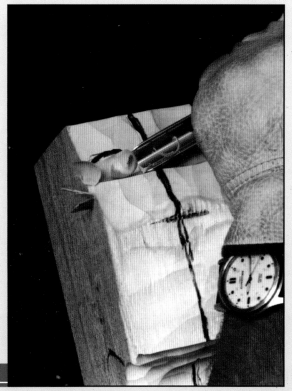

8

Using a #9, 15 mm or 13 mm gouge, make a cut straight across the brow ridge. This cut will start setting the deepest part of the face back in so the nose can start to take shape.

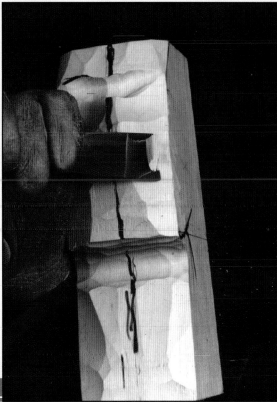

9

With a #5 gouge, push the side of the face back toward the secondary profile. This step is very important and will take care of any "flat face" problems that you might encounter. Be sure that you don't take the gouge up the side of the nose; otherwise you will be removing wood that you need for the structure of the face.

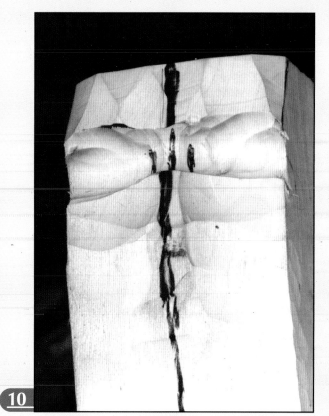

10

The two marks—one on each side of the bridge of the nose—locate the edge of the eye sockets. The gouge should come out of the cut at these points. Rough in the eye sockets with a #11, 10 mm or 12 mm gouge. Make sure to leave the wood between the eye sockets.

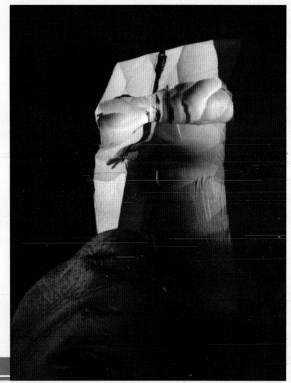

11

Using a #5, 10 mm or 15 mm gouge turned upside-down, create the initial profile of the nose. Start at the bottom of the nose and cut right up into the bridge.

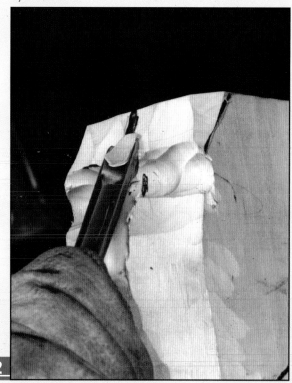

12

Split the brows with a #9, 13 mm gouge. This cut will put a dent in the middle of the eyebrow ridge.

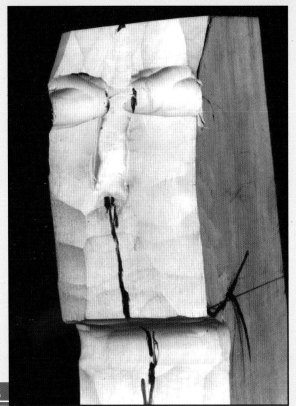

13

A three-quarter view of the face shows the effects of the cuts to this point.

14

Using the #5, 30 mm gouge, dig in on the sides of the nose to begin the cuts that will push the face back.

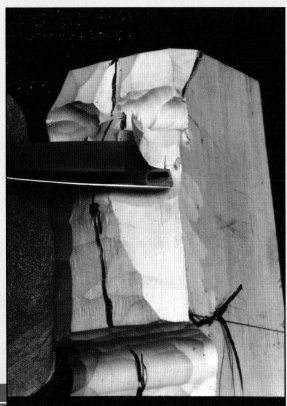

15

Follow through, taking the cut all the way to the edge of the face. Don't be bashful about taking some wood off here. Your goal is to bring the nose and the mouth barrel area forward by pushing the rest of the face back.

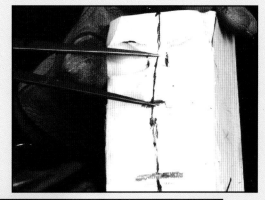

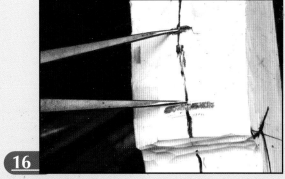

16

Measure from the bridge of the nose to the center of the nose. Keeping the same measurement on the calipers, move the calipers down to the center of the nose. The bottom leg of the calipers will mark the bottom of the chin. I am being pretty liberal on the bottom of the chin. I find it is better to leave just a little extra wood than to cut off too much wood right away.

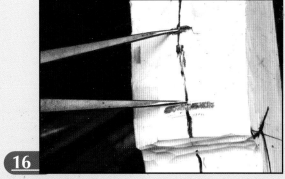

Native American

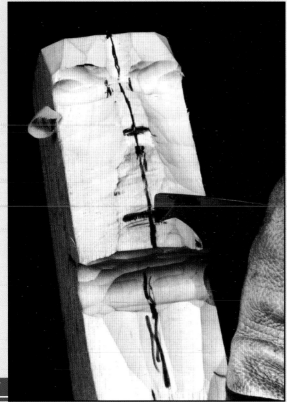

17

Remove all the wood below the dark line of the chin with a large #5 gouge.

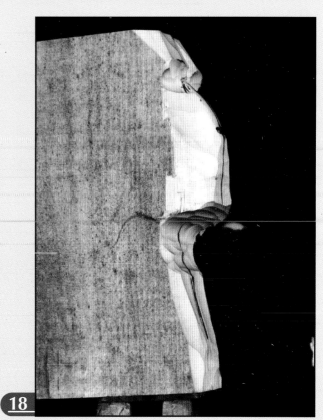

18

A side view of the piece shows the cuts to this point. Notice the smooth transition of form from the nose to the side of the face. Also notice how everything is marked in.

19

Draw in the approximate location of the cheekbones. These marks will be a guide point to keep the cheeks from getting too high or too low from one side to the other. Everything must be symmetrical.

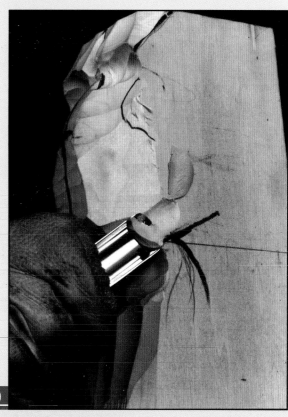

20

Work back to the jaw line with a big #9 gouge. Notice the gouge cut on the side of the face. That's about how deep the jaw should be cut into the block when the piece is done. Work across the neck and up the opposite side to create the three planes of the neck.

46 • Carving the Nose and Mouth

21

Using the #5 again, push the face back. Work underneath the cheekbones to rough in where the natural hollow of the face will be. The cheekbones and brow mask area are exaggerated a bit in sculptures of Native Americans. These areas are a lot heavier in Native Americans than in Caucasians and give distinction between the two races.

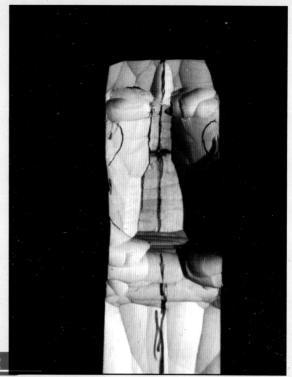

22

A front view of the face at this point shows the progress to this point. The cheekbones are roughly sketched in: They act as guidelines for shaping the rest of the face. Re-establish the centerline, the bottom of the nose and the cheek area.

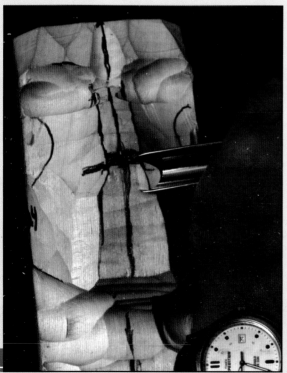

23

Using a #9, 13 mm gouge, make a good, hard cut right underneath the nose. Go straight across: Don't angle up or down. Notice how I'm dropping down a little lower than where I think the bottom of the nose might actually be. This extra wood will be cut off when the final cut at the end of the nose is made.

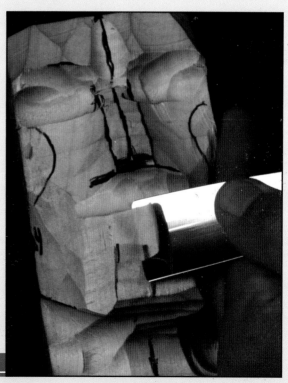

24

Push the mouth barrel back flush with the cut you made in the previous step. Round off the sharp edges on the chin area. These cuts create a good, strong dental curve.

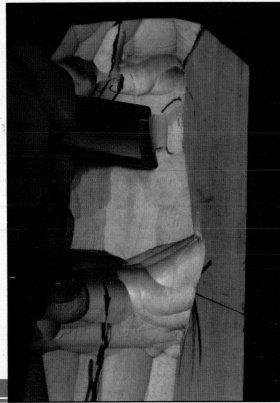

25

Remove small shavings of wood to create that smooth transition of form from the nose to the cheek. Again, you are pushing the cheek back.

26

Shape the top of the eye sockets with a #7, 14 mm gouge. The right side is done and I am working on the left side.

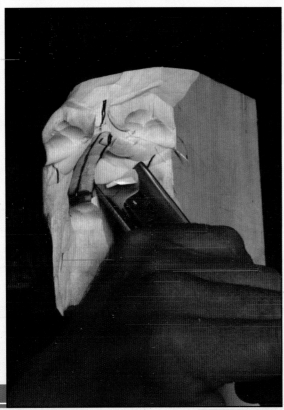

27

Use a #7, 3/4-inch gouge to give the area between the point of the cheekbone and the side of the nose a little bit of a hollow effect. This cut will create a stronger and smoother transition of form from the nose to the cheek.

28

A side view shows how the face has been pushed back to bring out the nose and the mouth area. The jaw line follows the same angle as the hour hand of a clock at 4 o'clock.

48 • Carving the Nose and Mouth

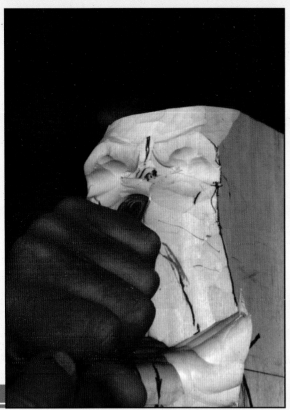

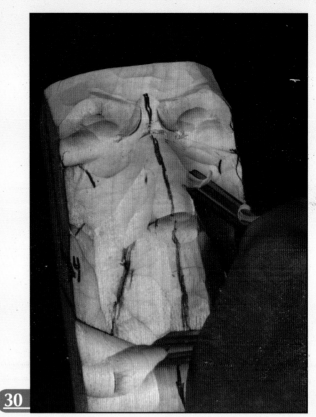

Finalize the profile of the nose. Turning a #7, 14 mm gouge upside-down, cut in the final profile of the nose. Let the corners dig in a little bit as this cut is made.

30

Here you can see the half-moon cut on the bridge of the nose where the gouge stopped. Now take a #7 up the side of the nose to create the hollow area below the nasal bone. Clean off the chip marks where the corner of the upside-down gouge dug into the wood.

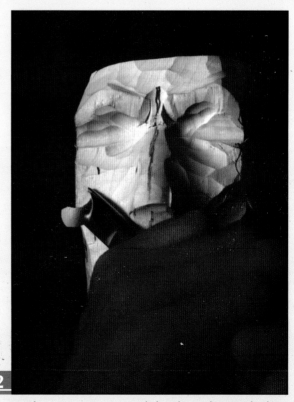

31

Deepen the eye sockets again. Using a #11, 10 mm gouge, make the three cuts that will shape the sockets. As with the Caucasian profile, it's important to work all over the face a little at a time so that all elements of the face will be finished together.

32

With a #7 gouge, work back underneath the bottom side of the cheekbone to create a hollow. Work at an upward angle, which tends to be the angle that the cheekbones follow.

Carving the Nose and Mouth • 49

Native American

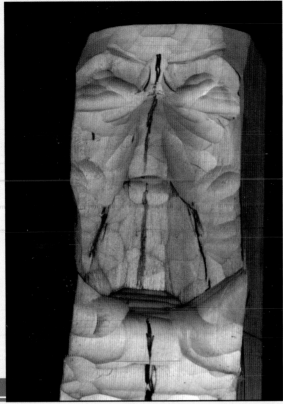

33

At this point, the face should look like this picture. The double diamonds have been established on the nose, the eye sockets are carved in, and the cheekbones are set. The face is now discernable as a Native American.

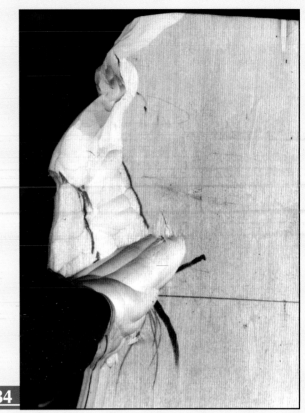

34

A side view shows the profile to this point. Notice the primary profile, the secondary profile and how the mouth barrel and the nose fit into the face. The cheekbone is protruding quite a bit; it will be dropped back a little later.

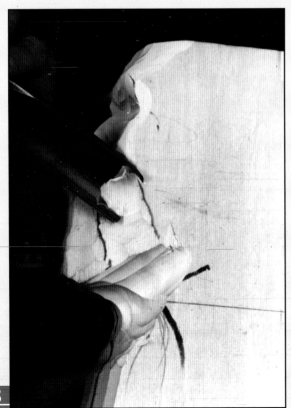

35

Refine the structure using a big #7, 3/4-inch gouge. Make a cut at a downward and backward angle into the wood underneath the cheekbone.

36

Push the chin back with a #7, 3/4-inch gouge. This cut will begin to define the mouth area.

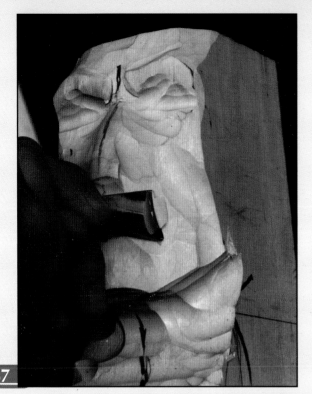

37

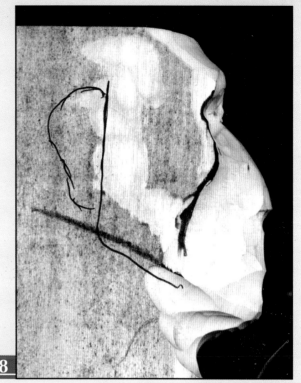

38

Now you have some blending to do. Blend the mouth barrel back at an outward angle with a #3, 1-inch gouge. Round off some of the sharp edges on the chin.

The face is taking shape. Notice the differences between the secondary profile and the primary profile. (The gouge marks on the side of the face show roughly how deep the face will be where the face meets the ear. Marking this in helps to give me perspective on the whole head, but it is optional for this demonstration.)

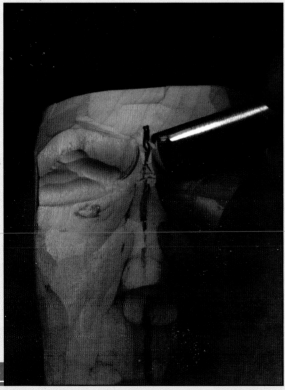

39

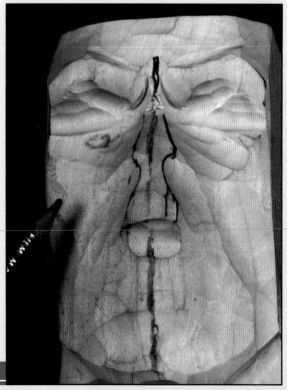

40

Refine the brow cut with a #7, 14 mm gouge. I have also shaped the nose up a bit more, enhancing the double-diamond effect.

This is as far as you need to take the eyes. Any additional shaping of the eyes would not affect the shape of the nose. The pencil is pointing to the hollow that goes down from the nose under the cheekbone and on around the face.

Carving the Nose and Mouth • 51

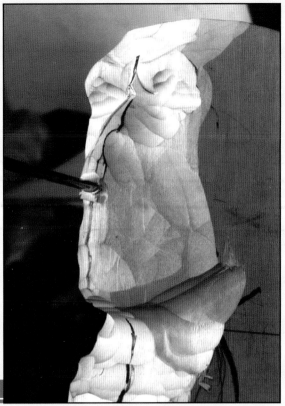

41

Now it's time to start finalizing the nose. Roll a #7, 10 mm gouge right down along the curvature of the nose and cut straight in to establish the center front of the nose. This cut will also finalize the bottom line of the nose.

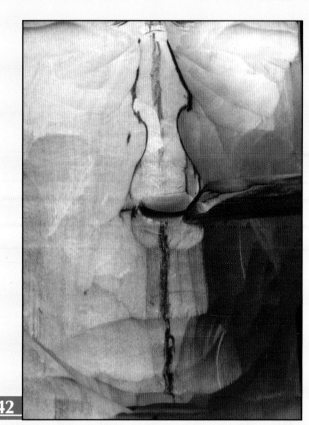

42

Swing the handle of the tool right around the base of the nose and make the cut to mark the side of the nose around the dental curve.

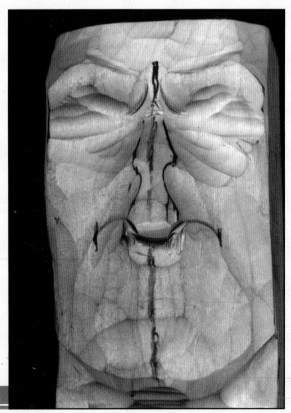

43

This photo shows what the nose looks like when all three cuts have been made to establish the bottom of the nose.

44

Using the #3, 1-inch gouge again, sweep back from the side of the nose right down to the cheekbone. This cut will define and strengthen the smooth transition of form between the nose and the chin.

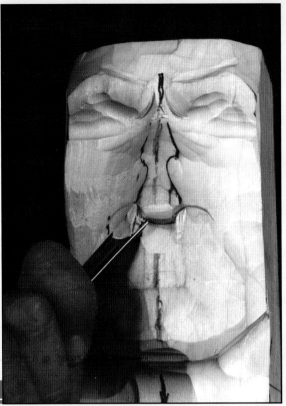

45

Relieve the wood under the cuts. The cut under the center of the nose has been made.

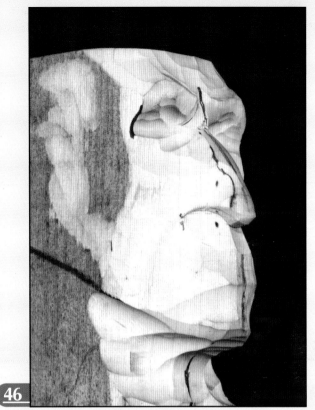

46

A side view shows all the cuts relieved. Notice how these cuts have caused the mouth area to become more pronounced.

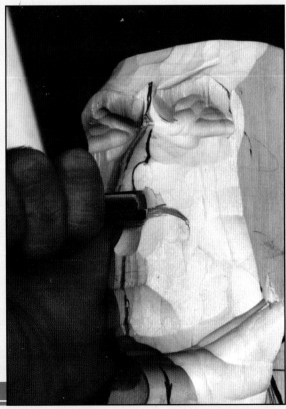

47

Turn a #7, 10 mm gouge upside-down for this step. Using only about one-half to three-quarters of the gouge's cutting edge, skate down the side of the nose at an outward angle.

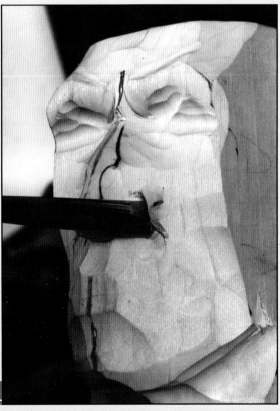

48

Stop here. A common mistake many people make is to not take enough wood or go deep enough. Don't be afraid to push in deep. That said, you don't want to pull the gouge to the right during this process. If you dig in behind the nostril the effect will be ruined.

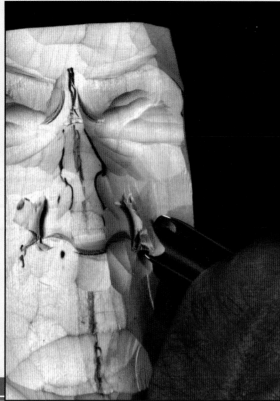

49

Relieve the wood with a #9, 13 mm gouge. Notice how the cuts have rounded the sides of the nose.

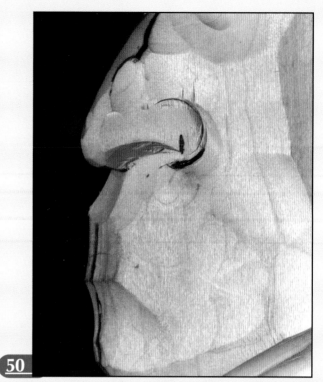

50

This shot shows how deep the nose goes into the face. It illustrates the rule that about half of the nose is off the face and half of the nose is on the face. Notice the two marks I've made: The vertical mark is the end of the cut that establishes the bottom of the nose; the other mark is where the nostril will curl around the nose. Very shapely, very prominent noses are another characteristic of Native American faces.

51

Relieve the wood around the nose with a #9 gouge; then deepen the area with the #11, as shown here.

52

A side view of the face shows how the cuts go back into the face and around the muscle area at the corner of the mouth.

54 • Carving the Nose and Mouth

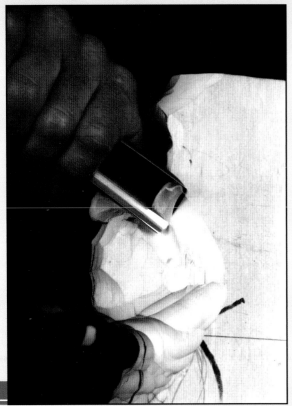

53 Using a #7, 3/4-inch gouge, carve above the smile line and under the cheekbone, creating that natural hollow in the face again.

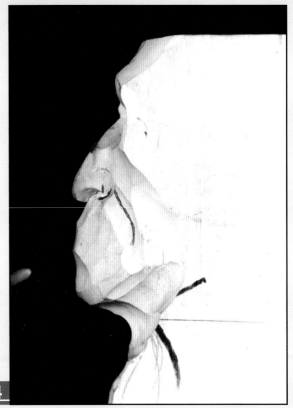

54 This side view shows a good shot of the side cuts that were made to hollow out the area under the cheekbone. Notice the good, strong profile of the nose and mouth area.

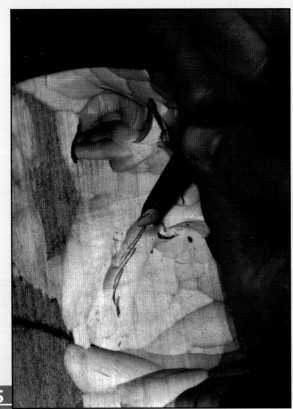

55 Pencil in a mark to show the smile line. With a #11, 5 mm gouge, shave down through the pencil mark.

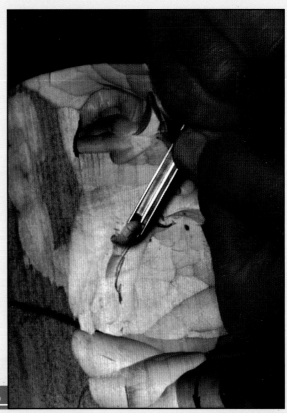

56 The cut continues down the face. Stop halfway down. Notice how the cut goes back into the face.

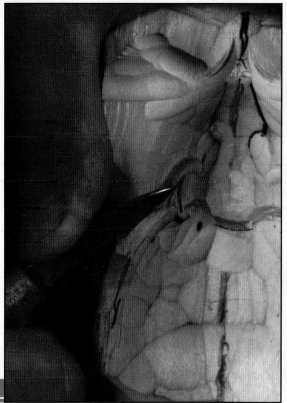

57

Holding a carving knife at about a 45-degree angle to the face, make a slicing cut around the mouth area.

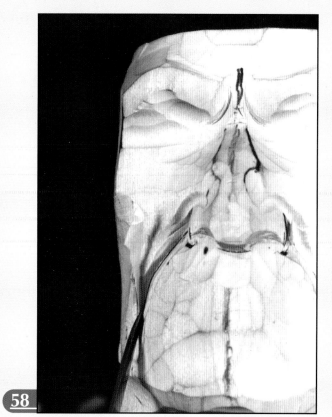

58

Flip the knife over and make the other side of the cut. Notice the piece of wood that falls out. It should fall out perfectly if you approach the angles correctly and if your knife is sharp.

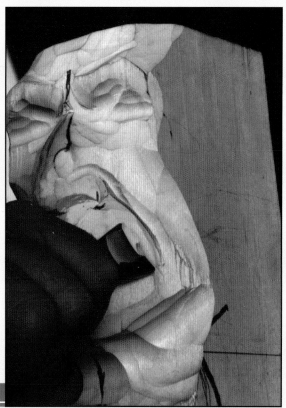

59

Blend the mouth into the smile line. Narrow the mouth barrel and work on the side plane with a #3, 1-inch gouge. "Tuck" everything right back into the smile line. Do not take big bites out of the wood to accomplish this step.

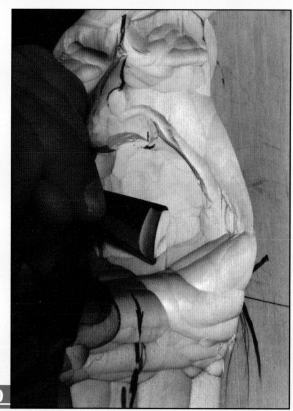

60

Narrow the chin area using the #3, 1-inch gouge.

56 • Carving the Nose and Mouth

61

Using a #11 gouge, begin to carve the nostril opening. Start the cut here at the back of the nostril and work toward the front.

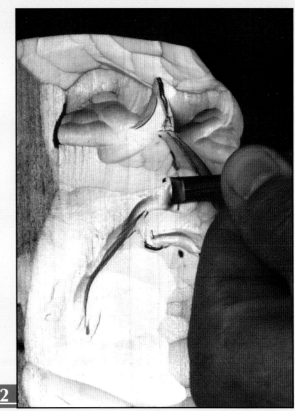

62

Use a #7 gouge to remove the sharp edges of the previous gouge cuts. Notice the shape of the finished nostril.

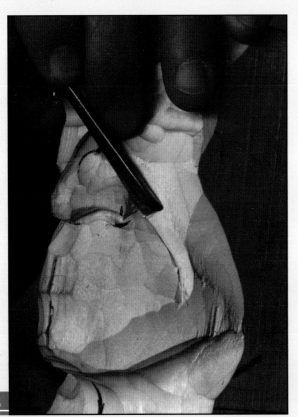

63

Flip the gouge upside-down and round off the sharp edge of the nasal labial fold. Approach this cut from the top. The correct angle will give the look of soft, folded skin.

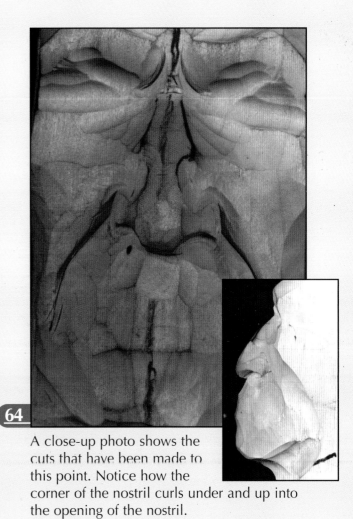

64

A close-up photo shows the cuts that have been made to this point. Notice how the corner of the nostril curls under and up into the opening of the nostril.

Carving the Nose and Mouth • 57

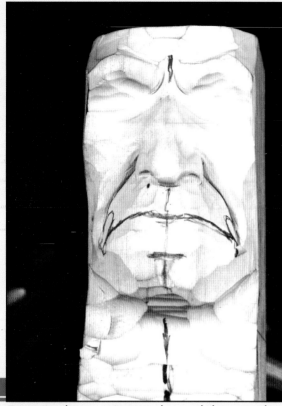

65 Draw in the corner muscles and the actual separation of the lips. The shorter horizontal line under the lips shows the separation of the chin from the mouth.

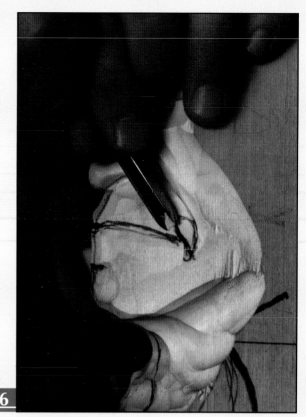

66 Create the muscle at the corner of the mouth by removing wood in front of the muscle with a #11, 5 mm gouge. The cut starts here and continues to the bottom of the pencil line.

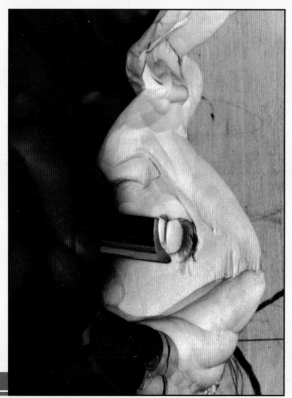

67 With a #5, 15 mm gouge, trim the mouth barrel. Be sure to stop the cut before the muscle. This creates a stair-step effect in this area: The cheek is the farthest out; the muscle is next; and then the corner of the mouth. As a general rule of thumb, the mouth of a Native American extends beyond the center of the eye.

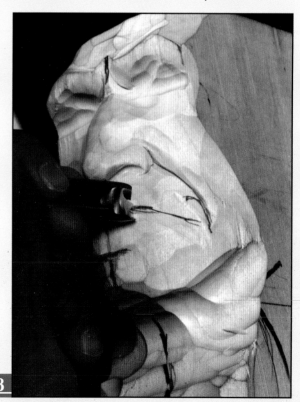

68 Using a #9, 10 mm or 13 mm gouge, make a cut along the mouth line. I start at the middle and work toward the corner.

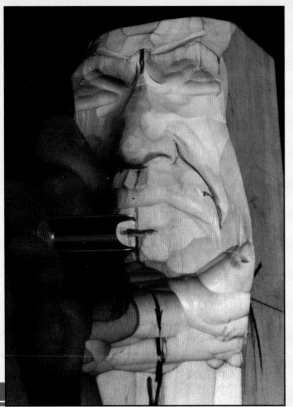

69 Using a #9, 10 mm or #9, 13 mm gouge, separate the mouth from the chin.

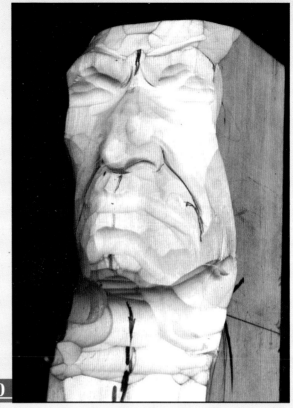

70 A three-quarter view shows the cuts of the mouth and chin. Notice the heavy wood left under the outside corner of the mouth below the bottom lip. That's another typical feature: Native Americans have a stronger musculature around that area.

71 Use a #5 or #7 gouge to smooth and blend in the sharp edges of the chin cut.

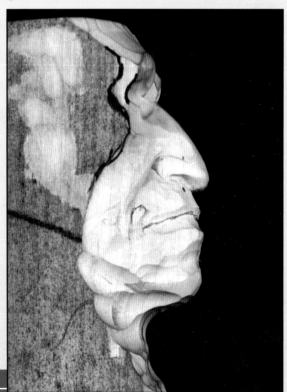

72 Draw in the mouth line for the next step. Notice how the chin is back behind the bottom lip a little bit. The chin is very round and protrudes strongly. This structure is what creates a prominent mouth on a Native American face.

Native American

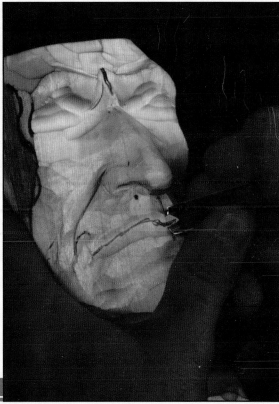

73

Using a 90-degree V-tool with a square shape, cut in the lips. Start the cut in the middle, do the little center curve, then come right on down to the corner of the mouth.

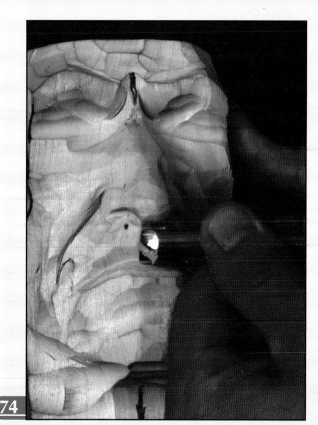

74

Broaden the top lip area with an upside-down #5 or #7 gouge. Don't remove a lot of wood or make the cut any deeper—just round the sharp edge off. This will make the lip exceptionally fat. Make these cuts on both sides of the mouth, working from the center out.

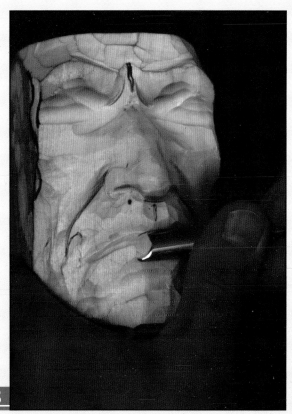

75

Repeat this procedure on the lower lip as well.

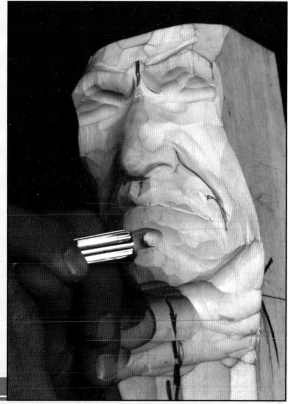

76

Separate the chin from the mouth using a #9 gouge. Cut across and down through the previous chin cut. Continue to roll that cut right around and up behind the smile line into the natural hollow of the cheek.

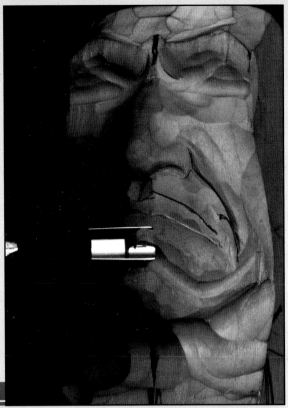

77

Using the #7 gouge, start in the center and work toward the outside corner to form the bottom edge of the bottom lip. Remember, the bottom lip tucks underneath the top lip.

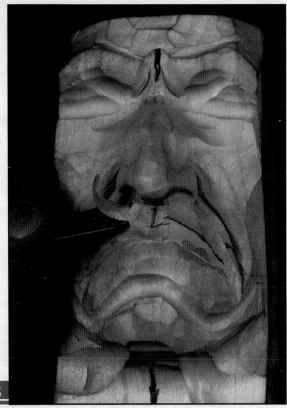

78

Remove wood from the top of the lips. Notice the sharp edge of the top and bottom lips and the crease between the two.

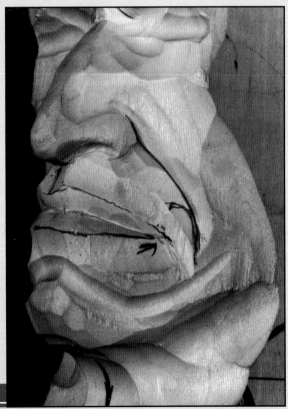

79

Here I have sketched in the edges that were created. Notice how the bottom lip tucks up underneath the top lip. Study this shot. A correctly carved mouth should match this example.

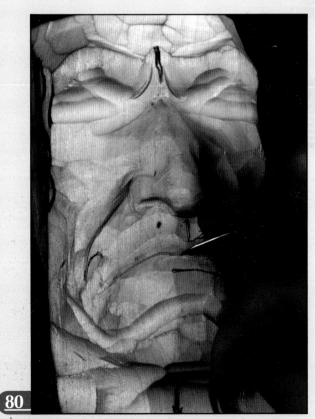

80

Open the mouth up a bit with a carving knife. Outline the top lip by cutting fairly straight in.

Carving the Nose and Mouth • 61

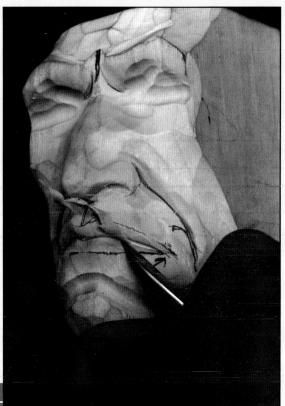

81

Complete the cut by cutting in at an angle to meet the first cut. If the angles are correct and your knife is sharp, a small shaving will pop right out.

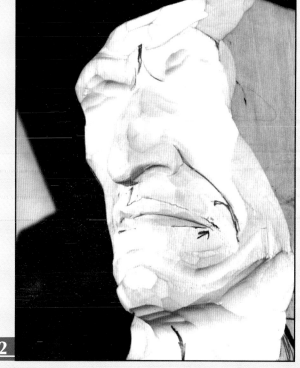

82

A three-quarter view shows the finished lips. Notice the outer profile of the corner of the face on the left-hand side. Look specifically at the strong bony cheekbone structure and the eyebrow structure. The shapes of these features are common to Native American faces.

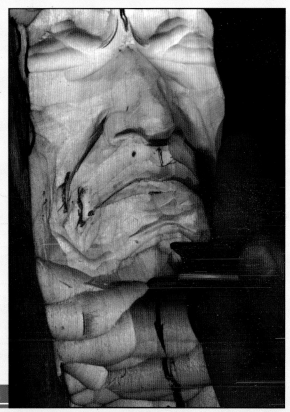

83

Put in the cleft of the chin with a #5, 10 mm to 13 mm gouge. Start the cut by pushing in slightly. Notice the angle of the gouge. Now, hold the gouge in place and twist it down toward the neck.

84

Notice the final shape of the cleft in the chin. Using a #9, 13 mm gouge, start a cut to create some muscle structure in the cheek area.

Diagram 14

Eye Socket Differences

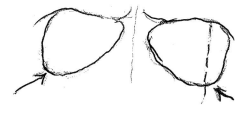

Caucasian Shape

Notice how the lowest part of the socket is toward the outside.

Native American Shape

Notice the lowest part of the socket is toward the center of the socket. This is due to the heavy cheek bone structure that is lacking in Caucasians.

Diagram 15

Wrinkle Patterns

Notice the wrinkle pattern. All of the wrinkles follow the contours and muscle groups of the face.

Diagram 16

Aging Process

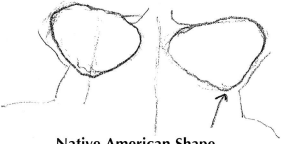

End of nasal bone

Cartilage

As age sets in, the cartilage at the end of the nasal bone begins to break down causing a "dent" in the profile of the nose, allowing the ball of the nose to fall.

Aging of the mouth tends to allow the line of the lips to fall from one third of the way between the nose and chin to almost halfway between the nose and chin. With age, lips tend to thin and pucker, creating wrinkles around the lip area that conform to the contour of the shape and muscles in that area.

SUBSCRIBE TODAY!

DON'T MISS ANOTHER ISSUE OF SCROLL SAW WORKSHOP

☐ **ONE YEAR** Subscription

☐ $19.95 USA
☐ $22.50 Canada - US Funds Only
☐ $27.95 Int'l - US Funds Only

☐ **TWO YEAR** Subscription

☐ $39.90 USA
☐ $45.00 Canada - US Funds Only
☐ $55.90 Int'l - US Funds Only

Please allow 4-6 weeks for delivery

Four issues per year

☐ Bill Me   ☐ Check/Money Order
☐ Visa, MC or Discover

Name on card _____
Exp. date _____ Telephone ( ) _____
cardnumber
☐☐☐☐☐☐☐☐☐☐☐☐☐☐☐☐

Send To:

Name: _____
Address: _____
_____
City: _____
State/Prov.: _____
Zip: _____
Telephone: _____ Country: _____

VISA MasterCard DISCOVER NOVUS   CFBN

FREE
with a two-year
paid subscription

Subscription order desk 888-840-8590

SUBSCRIBE TODAY!

DON'T MISS ANOTHER ISSUE OF WOOD CARVING ILLUSTRATED

☐ **ONE YEAR** Subscription

☐ $19.95 USA
☐ $22.50 Canada - US Funds Only
☐ $27.95 Int'l - US Funds Only

☐ **TWO YEAR** Subscription

☐ $39.90 USA
☐ $45.00 Canada - US Funds Only
☐ $55.90 Int'l - US Funds Only

Please allow 4-6 weeks for delivery

Four issues per year

☐ Bill Me   ☐ Check/Money Order
☐ Visa, MC or Discover

Name on card _____
Exp. date _____ Telephone ( ) _____
cardnumber
☐☐☐☐☐☐☐☐☐☐☐☐☐☐☐☐

Send To:

Name: _____
Address: _____
_____
City: _____
State/Prov.: _____
Zip: _____
Telephone: _____ Country: _____

VISA MasterCard DISCOVER NOVUS   CFBN

FREE
with a two-year
paid subscription

Subscription order desk: 888-506-6630

FREE BOOK CATALOG

YES! *I'd like a free catalog of your woodworking titles. Please place me on your mailing list and send me a copy right away.*

Previously purchased titles:
_____
_____

I'm particularly interested in: *(circle all that apply)*   General Woodworking   Woodcarving   Scroll Sawing   Cabinetmaking   Nature Drawing

Suggestion box: I think Fox Chapel should do a book about:
_____

Bonus: Give us your email address to receive free updates.

Send to:
Name: _____   Email Address: _____
Address: _____   City: _____
State/Prov.: _____
Telephone: _____ Country: _____   Zip: _____

**Visit us on the web at www.Foxchapelpublishing.com
or call us at 800-457-9112**

AFB00

Scroll Saw Work Shop
The How-To Magazine for Scrollers

1970 Broad St.
East Petersburg PA 17520   USA

Wood Carving
I L L U S T R A T E D

1970 Broad St.
East Petersburg PA 17520   USA

Fox Chapel Publishing Co. Inc.

Free Catalog Offer
1970 Broad St.
East Petersburg PA 17520   USA